BIG
DATA
MARKETING

John —

To my favorite,
data-driven
PR rock star!
Thanks for
all you do

Love,
[signature]
10.20.13

BIG DATA MARKETING

ENGAGE YOUR CUSTOMERS
MORE EFFECTIVELY
AND DRIVE VALUE

LISA ARTHUR

WILEY

For general information about our other products and services, please contact our
Customer Care Department within the United States at (800) 762-2974, outside the United
States at (317) 572-3993 or fax (317) 572-4002.

Wiley publishes in a variety of print and electronic formats and by print-on-demand. Some
material included with standard print versions of this book may not be included in e-books
or in print-on-demand. If this book refers to media such as a CD or DVD that is not
included in the version you purchased, you may download this material at
http://booksupport.wiley.com. For more information about Wiley products, visit
www.wiley.com.

ISBN: 978-1-118-73389-9 (cloth)
ISBN: 978-1-118-73402-5 (ebk)
ISBN: 978-1-118-73405-6 (ebk)

Printed in the United States of America.
10 9 8 7 6 5 4 3 2 1

For my love, my muse, and my true north, Michael Bloom.
For my butterfly mom, Betty Burris.

Contents

Foreword

Why did you get into marketing? I am guessing that it's not because you had a burning desire to refine propensity models until the wee hours of the morning, or to wrestle with integrating social media comments with web clickstream data. But those are exactly the kinds of activities that make marketers great these days. The function is undergoing a dramatic transformation toward a world of data-driven decisions that this book describes in detail. You may have gravitated toward marketing because it is one of the most creative areas of business, and you still need to possess that attribute to succeed. But creativity is increasingly judged not only in the human imagination, but also in clickthroughs, conversions, and lift.

Marketing is not, of course, the only area of business undergoing this transformation. Few people enter the retail industry because they have a fascination with point-of-sale data, and few baseball fans want to work for a team so they can compute its Pythagorean winning percentage. The world in general is becoming more data-driven, and the change in marketing is only one example of that overall shift.

However, as Lisa Arthur details in the chapters that follow, the change in marketing is especially dramatic. In little more than a decade, the function has gone from emphasizing pretty pictures and catchy phrases to one that captures, integrates, and analyzes data of all types. Needless to say, many marketers—and the managers outside the function who relate to marketers—are not quite prepared for this transformation. They've heard the noise about data-driven marketing, but they're hoping they can retire before they really have to change their entire orientation.

But unless they're well into their sixties, retirement won't help much. Every day, marketing assets become increasingly digitized. Every day, more information about customers' preferences and behaviors becomes available. Every day, the opportunity cost of not pursuing data-driven marketing piles up.

There is both an organizational and an individual imperative for reading this book, internalizing its lessons, and continuing the pursuit of data-driven marketing. At the organizational level, some group of people needs to take the lead within companies in moving toward a data and analytics-focused culture. Marketing, as the function most impacted by the rise of data—and as the most frequent gatherer and user of customer data—is in an excellent position to take the lead and to lead by example. If marketing can target customer promotions, understand the attribution of digital media to sales, and segment to markets of one, the rest of the organization can't help but move in the same data-driven direction.

If marketing takes the lead in this regard, it can also seize an opportunity to take primary responsibility for managing customer interaction data. As you probably realize, marketing is not the only customer-oriented function in most organizations. It shares that responsibility with sales and customer service. My view is that over the next several years, organizations will feel the need to clarify who is really responsible for customer information. If marketing groups can demonstrate that they are adept at managing and using customer information—and making the data accessible to other organizations that need it—there's a good chance that marketing will get the role for the entire organization.

Of course, in order to do that successfully, marketing will need to step up its professionalism in data management. As Arthur points out, that means discipline, a process orientation, and lots of work on data integration. These are not generally traits that are traditionally associated with marketing, so some changes need to be made. Arthur refers to the prediction by Gartner that by the year 2017, marketing organizations will spend more on technology than IT organizations. I am not sure that prediction will come true (and even less sure it will happen on this date), but if it's even close, marketing data management will have to adopt some of the same approaches to data hygiene (security, backup, version control, and so forth) that IT organizations have employed for decades.

There is some irony in the move by marketing into professionally managed information and technology. Over the years, marketers have frequently been guilty of a "renegade" approach to IT. Instead of working with the IT function to create a professional approach to data management, marketers often tried to evade scrutiny by acquiring technology and managing complex data environments on their own. The marketers in question may well have gotten their database up or analyzed their social media sentiments more quickly and inexpensively. However, this renegade approach has led to fragmented and siloed customer data, as well as some inefficiencies in technology architecture and platform management.

Going forward, it's not that marketing will replace IT in the professional management of data, but will collaborate with it. Indeed, one organization—Arthur's own firm, Teradata—recently combined the jobs of chief marketing officer (CMO) and chief information officer (CIO). Perhaps we will see more such combinations, but in any case we will certainly need to see collaboration. Whenever I meet CMOs who don't work closely with their companies' CIOs, I consider shorting their stock. I can't imagine the companies will be successful if marketing and IT don't get along.

At the individual level, it's now clear that marketers at every level need to embrace technology and data as key elements of their professional portfolios. Everyone needs to know something; some need to know a lot. Every individual marketer needs to stake out a position on the continuum that has traditional, creative, intuitive marketing on one end (a position that is no longer tenable by itself), and hard-core digital data management on the other. If you're on the extreme data-oriented end, you may not look much different from a traditional IT person, although you will happen to specialize in managing customer-oriented data.

Some marketers will need to go back for formal schooling to develop this expertise; others can get by, as Arthur notes, with internal skill development programs within companies. Highly self-motivated individuals may even be able to acquire the needed knowledge by studying the voluminous amount of online information on this topic. Whatever means you choose, acquiring this sort of knowledge takes hard work.

And in marketing, the work to keep up with expanding IT and big data knowledge won't stop for the foreseeable future. It's great that you are reading this book, and Arthur will have provided you with a solid foundation for big data marketing by the time you reach its end. However, the world of data-driven marketing is changing at a dramatic pace. New channels to the customer, new application categories, new types of data to exploit, and new vendors and offerings emerge all the time. To be successful in data-driven marketing, you'll have to become a student of this domain for the rest of your career.

This may seem daunting, but try to look at it as a fantastic time to be in this profession. What could be more stimulating than being in a part of business where the foundations are being shaken on a daily basis? Where better to be than in the vanguard of this change? Wouldn't you prefer to be a leader of this transformation than to be led by someone else? In short, it's a wonderful time to be a data-driven marketer if you like change, excitement, and new ideas. And if you don't like those things, marketing probably isn't the best place for you anyway!

—Thomas H. Davenport

Acknowledgments

First, I'd like to acknowledge you, the reader of this book. Thank you for helping eliminate the hype and mystery from big data and data-driven marketing. Since all profits from the sale of this book will be donated to the American Red Cross, I am also sincerely grateful for your purchase. The American Red Cross is an organization passionate about its donors and the lives they save, and I am extremely proud that together we're contributing to the success of that mission.

I'd also like to say thank you to all the marketers I've met and shared stories with over the years. You inspired me to write this book, as we stand at the dawn of the Enlightened Age of Data. Let's keep talking and working together to elevate our teams and how we engage with customers; then, the rest will be history, as the saying goes.

I owe infinite gratitude and professional kudos to two brilliant women who came together with me to complete this project. Kathy Siranosian, you are an amazing partner in crime. This book would still be an outline and a dream if it weren't for your positive spirit, your tireless contributions, and your talent in translating my stories into compelling chapters. Applause and crowd noise also go to Kelly Jones, who researched and wrote case studies under extreme deadlines and continually contributed a fresh perspective. Thank you, content mavens, both your names should be alongside mine on the jacket. Another shout-out goes to Paige O'Neill, who helped outline the book, Christy Uher-Ferguson for her early reviews and feedback, and Mary Gros for helping secure the best thought leaders out there! What a powerful team of women and brainpower we have!

A *big thank-you* goes out to Teradata Corporation. Darryl McDonald, the president of Teradata Applications, and my manager, never blinked an eye when I asked to write this book while working as our chief marketing officer. Additional big thanks to Bill Franks, Ed Dupee, Gerald Hardister, David Scwheer, Lauren Ames, Dana Chamberlain, Wes Moore, Sherri Morgan, John Sawyer, Katherine Knowles, Tina Watkins, and Julyn Farrington, who all helped make this book happen. Even though there were many nights and weekends when I wondered if I was crazy for attempting this project on such a short deadline, I knew I had the backing and support of the Teradata team.

I'd be remiss if I didn't thank my Wiley editors, Adrianna Johnson and Christine Moore. Adrianna, you have been a beacon of light managing this process, a first time for me. Above and beyond navigating the publishing world, both you and Christine provided insightful edits and guidance to help my words truly resonate. Thank you and everyone at Wiley for such a robust and productive partnership.

To the strong women in my life, I wouldn't be here without you. To my mother, Betty Burris, my sister, Rebecca Davis, and my former executive coach, Debi Mueller: Thank you for all your love, wisdom, and support. Likewise, a sincere thank-you to my brother, Bob Burris, and adopted brother Lee Zeidman, who taught me how to be me in a man's world.

Finally, I count myself the luckiest woman in the world to share my life and passions with my husband, partner, and writing inspiration, Michael Bloom. Michael, a writer as well, continues to be my secret weapon professionally, as well as a source of ideation—and extraordinary coffee—when I need fuel to keep going. Thanks, my love, for your brutal honesty, your laser insight, and your understanding, even when my Eric Clapton T-shirt (which I frequently wear when I write) stayed on just a little bit too long! Michael, you are a true and equal partner. I wouldn't be able to do what I do without you.

Introduction

Big *data*. I've been a marketer since 1984, and never have there been two words that cause more anguish in the C-suite. Over the years, I've seen corporate leaders execute masterful acquisitions, heroic management of budget cuts, aggressive staffing reductions, and other feats of strength. They seem to take most business hurdles more or less in stride, but mention the words *big data*, and the conversation changes. Every member of the C-suite agrees big data is an issue that needs immediate attention. The problem is, very few know what to do about it, and, of course, that indecision just adds to the anxiety. As companies put off formulating their plans, the data continues to stream in, creating massive tangles of information, processes, and applications. The knot grows. Insights and value get buried in all the chaos. Stomachs begin to ache. And no one wants to admit they're falling farther and farther behind.

I want to change that dynamic, and I wrote this book because it's time to open up the conversation about big data. As uncomfortable as it may be, we need to start discussing big data—the good, the bad, and the ugly—without hype, without sales pitches, and without fear. Today's business leaders need to roll up their sleeves and confront the challenge of big data head-on, but in order to do so, they must first have a clear view of the task ahead of them. I truly believe that kind of clarity can only be achieved through honest, real-world dialogue. That's why this book isn't filled with complex mathematical models and lists of confusing statistics. Instead, I chose to focus on what I've discovered as a marketer who's coming of age in the era of big data marketing. I wrote about my mistakes and successes, as well as the triumphs of those I have had the pleasure to learn from along the way. You'll find page after page of practical advice about how to drive the changes required to begin reaping the benefits of big data insights.

If you want your business to move forward, if you're tired of all the sensationalism and hype, if you're ready to ease that knot in your stomach, you've come to the right place. Turn the page. Let's start the conversation.

The Problem

How Did We Get Here?

1

Moving Out of the Dark Ages

More and more, the C-suite feels like a goat rodeo, a chaotic arena of business executives talking over and past one another. In fact, this pandemonium of different agenda and perceptions is now the spectator sport characterizing the Dark Ages of business. Even worse, it often takes only two of us to get the rodeo started.

I've seen this firsthand. One afternoon, while I was working as a chief marketing officer (CMO) at a Silicon Valley technology start-up, I seized the opportunity to talk to the CEO about how we could improve our demand creation and solution adoption. After briefly explaining that more resources would help us segment our market and buyers, I began to lay out my strategy for developing different content and engagement strategies for each unique persona, but, just as I was hitting my stride, the CEO interrupted me.

He was operationally focused, and already, he had heard enough. He looked me straight in the eye. "We don't need to segment the market," he said. "We just need to market."

Instantly, I knew I had failed. I hadn't effectively communicated *why* improving connections and conversations with customers and prospects would add value to the business. Clearly, the CEO didn't understand that messages and offers targeted to different buying personas would yield more eyeballs, more conversions to free trials, and ultimately, more paid subscriptions of software. And since I couldn't provide quantitative proof of the returns from my suggested plan, he certainly wasn't willing to devote any more resources. I knew we needed to invest in data analysis to better understand the market and advance our overall strategy and marketing techniques, but, to this CEO, that request was out of the question.

At the time, I was frustrated. Why didn't he *get it*? Worse, I wasn't sure how—and even *if*—I could help him understand.

Unfortunately, clashes and fly-bys like this happen every day in C-suites and boardrooms around the globe. They're all too common, and they're indicative of the chasm now separating marketing from the rest of the enterprise. On one side, there are the marketers who understand the intrinsic value of heightened customer engagement. On the other, there are the C-level execs who need to secure funding, drive change, and ease the organization's growing pains—the very aches caused by fragmented data, fragmented systems, and disconnected interaction channels.

Of course, marketers have been envisioning one-to-one relationships with customers for decades. They've always been the consumers' champions, advocating within the C-suite not only for better customer service and support, but also for product developments. When *The One to One Future*, a book by Don Peppers and Martha Rogers, was first published in 1993, it captivated the industry by focusing on the individual customer rather than the market as a whole. This book became the marketer's bible, inspiring new customer relationship strategies and insights into ways to better engage through true one-to-one experiences.

Since then, however, marketers have struggled to make the relevant, targeted, and value-based conversations they have promised real for most brands and their buyers. Even though consumers are clamoring for a more modern approach, the majority of companies continue to deliver just the opposite. From my perspective, that's no surprise. Outdated, ineffective, and ad hoc internal marketing processes, coupled with fragmented and missing data, can only lead to flat, one-size-fits-all messaging and interactions. And these lackluster experiences, in turn, are creating another gap, one that's particularly perilous because it separates brands from their customers at a time when consumer patience is growing thin. How much wider will these chasms grow? How much longer can we stand at the edge of the cliff, secretly hoping the disconnects will somehow resolve themselves?

The Threat of Digital Disruption

We can't wait anymore. A new vision of customer engagement, one that's grounded in personalized, relevant, and consistent communication, must materialize. I'm not talking about simply segmenting markets and targeting messages. I'm appealing to brands to begin true one-to-one interactions with their buyers and prospects. We must market like we communicate in our everyday lives, as one individual to another, as well as to groups or segments. We have to embrace a two-pronged approach that drives highly relevant, individualized engagements, while also leveraging broader segmentations when it is cost effective and *good enough*. We have to imagine how a personalized experience with our brand, product, or service will benefit and add value to our customers. We have to build that experience, and we have to deliver it—*now*.

Why the urgency? Because companies are facing continued consumer pressure to step-up with compelling experiences *now*—before the competition does—and because today, digital disruption threatens virtually all business models, physical products, and value chain relationships. But what exactly is digital disruption?

Just like most of you, I've been trying to wrap my head around the concept. It's multifaceted, all-encompassing, and difficult to distill into a single sound bite. But, I'll do my best to explain. Here's my definition of digital disruption and what it means to business today: Just as the word "disruption" describes throwing convention into confusion, "digital disruption" describes how technology and data are changing our culture, throwing communication and the physical world of processes and goods into disorder, across all industries.

Every board, every CEO, every CMO—essentially every business executive I talk to—dreads the threat of digital disruption. I've even heard some Fortune 100 executives say they avoid using the term "disruption" when trying to drive change within their companies because the word alone ends up instilling fear rather than motivation.

But, won't validating this fear by ignoring digital disruption cause even more damage? Yes, it will.

As author and business advisor Shelly Palmer told me, no matter what business you're in, your company needs to think strategically about digital disruption. Its impact can be felt everywhere—business-to-business (B2B), business-to-consumer (B2C), supply side, demand side—no business can escape the relentless pace of technological change.[1] According to Palmer, who wrote *Digital Wisdom: Thought Leadership for a Connected World*, companies need to fail fast, fail cheap, and iterate. Long planning cycles have a place, but given the speed that information travels and the dramatic changes in consumer behaviors empowered by technology, an annual or even quarterly review of strategy and execution may be too stagnant. Companies must adopt more flexible and iterative approaches to planning because, as Palmer points out, "the rate of technological change will never be slower than it is today."

In other words, we are entering uncharted waters. "It took 30 years to connect the first two billion people to the Internet; it will take about eight years to connect the next two billion," Palmer said. "This unprecedented level of connectivity will empower new consumer behaviors. Companies and their leaders must adapt, or die!"

Where is digital disruption taking us? The answer will vary from sector to sector. As of this year, 3-D printers can produce a pair of designer sunglasses, an electric guitar body, and even human tissue. This simple example illustrates digital disruption within the manufacturing and durable goods industry where we are moving away from mass production into personalized reproduction. In financial services, digital upstarts and smartphones are challenging the future of banking relationships. Retailers are also navigating disruption as the focus moves from online-only retailers to the impact of omnichannel commerce and the accelerating role of mobile commerce. While some business leaders look to other industries to understand digital disruption, most are wrestling with their own business model threats. Think about it: As consumer power grows, not only are customers controlling the market conversation; they're bound to demand more control of their personal data, as well. The companies that thrive will be the ones that deliver value by building individual relationships with buyers based on trust and shared experiences. Digital disruption will connect business and consumers in new ways, and the winning companies will be the ones that scale the ability to transact with the individual.

Clearly, it's time for all of us—especially marketers—to move past the fear so we can confront digital disruption head on. Why especially marketers? Because marketing has been affected most by the explosion of digital channels and changes to consumer behavior. Plus, marketers are among those who stand to benefit the most from understanding the customer better through data analysis.

After all, digital disruption is not, by definition, a negative occurrence; it is a phenomenon that forces change. Companies can use digital disruption as the imperative to engage customers differently with more personalized, tailored, and data-driven messages across all points of interaction.

The Enlightened Age of Data

How is your company reacting to digital disruption? Do you agree that the C-suite needs to move from the Dark Ages into an Enlightened Age of

Data? Do you believe as I do that marketing needs to lead the way? As I mentioned earlier, marketers have long been the voice of customers within the enterprise, and now CEOs and the rest of the C-suite are counting on marketing to find new sources of revenue and differentiation through more compelling customer engagement and experiences. How should marketers respond?

Marketers must respond by using, leveraging, and applying *data*: Data from customers. Data from prospects. Data from warehouses. Partner data. Sensor data from durable goods. Competitive data. Internal data. External data. All of these data insights can be leveraged to create a competitive advantage. First, companies need to create more holistic views of their data. Then, they need to analyze that information for actionable insights. Finally, they need to put the processes and tools in place that enable them to execute based on those insights.

The bottom line? Marketing needs to be data driven. Let me be more precise. I define data-driven marketing as collecting, analyzing, and executing on insights from structured and multi-structured data (that is, big data) across the enterprise to drive customer engagement. Data-driven marketing is the engine behind improved marketing results, and it creates measurable internal accountability as marketers become more effective in planning, executing, and proving the value of their work.

And keep in mind: Using data to guide and inform does more than engage current customers. Data-driven marketing techniques also capture new customers. In 2011, the Information Technology Services Marketing Association's (ITSMA's) survey results showed that 82 percent of data-savvy marketers report greater market share[2] when using insights to drive marketing. That's proof that more targeted, relevant experiences pay off. Teradata Corporation found similar results in its 2013 survey of more than 1,000 marketers globally. The report, *Global Teradata Data-Driven Marketing Survey, 2013*, concludes that six out of ten marketers (58 percent) believe that a data-driven marketing approach helps them make better decisions.[3] (The complete report is available as a supplemental resource to this book at www.teradata.com/big-data-marketing or at www.bigdatamarketingbook.com.) Figure 1.1 shows how data-driven marketing impacts the overall field of marketing.

Kelly Cook, Senior Vice President of Marketing at Designer Shoe Warehouse (DSW), has seen it happen. When her team needed to rein-vigorate the DSW brand and drive growth for shareholders, Cook led

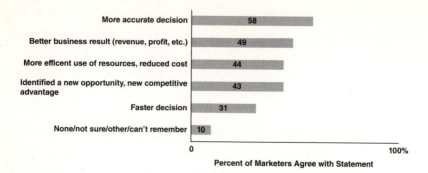

FIGURE 1.1 Benefits of Using Data in Making Decisions

Source: © 2013 "Teradata Data-Driven Marketing Survey, Global" Teradata Corporation.

a data-driven process to chart the consumer journey and deliver more personalized experiences in campaigns, offers, and messages.

"You need a fully integrated strategy being championed from the top of the house," Cook told *Teradata Magazine*. "Then it's just a matter of prioritizing all the things you need to do because believe me, customers have no problem telling you everything you could do better. Knowing what you need to do for customers allows you to understand what data is needed, so you'll know what to attack first."[4]

I believe all marketers must be open to this kind of reorientation. We're in the midst of a renaissance, of sorts, because a cultural shift is necessary to unify, understand, and leverage the enterprise and big data insights needed to drive more compelling, relevant customer engagement across all channels in real-time.

Of course, that's not to say that finding traction amidst all the disruption will be effortless, or even easy. Historians tell us that the Renaissance was a period characterized by inquiry, creativity, and growth juxtaposed with misunderstanding—and even fear—of innovators and their new points of view. I fully expect to see similar dynamics shape the Enlightened Age of Data, as the function of marketing continues to mature. During this renaissance, we're all bound to face skepticism from other smart and seasoned business leaders. Difficult new questions will force us to rethink the very ways we work to build our brands.

Before we move further ahead into the Enlightened Age of Data, let's take a closer look at what's been holding us back.

KEY TERMS

Data-driven marketing: Data-driven marketing is collecting, analyzing, and executing on insights from structured and multi-structured data (for example, big data) across the enterprise to drive customer engagement. Data-driven marketing is the engine behind improved marketing results and creates measurable internal accountability as marketers become more effective in planning, executing, and proving the value of marketing.

Digital disruption: The word "disruption" describes throwing convention into confusion, and "digital disruption" describes how technology and data are changing our culture, throwing communication and the physical world of processes and goods into disorder, across all industries.

Big data: Big data is composed of digital information, including unstructured and multi-structured data, often derived from inter-actions between people and machines such as web applications, social networks, genomics, and sensors. Big data is a continuous stream of information conducive for ongoing discovery and analysis. Industry leaders, like the global analyst firm Gartner[5], use adjectives like "velocity, and variety" as a way to frame the big data discussion.

DOs and DON'Ts

Recognize that the world has changed, and therefore the expectations of marketing have changed. For example, social media is here to stay, mobile is exploding in importance, and customers are savvy, smart, and in control.

Learn to leverage tension in the C-suite to inspire change. Healthy tension can identify the obstacles to charting

(continued)

(*continued*)

a new course and help you discover better ways to approach old problems. Avoid adding to the goat-rodeo dynamic. Instead, use the debates to build buy-in and alignment.

Commit to moving from the Dark Ages into the Enlightened Age of Data. Embrace the journey to a data-driven marketing organization, one that directs programs and spend with insights based on real-time market response. Then, develop a simple plan to move forward.

Don't assume digital disruption is someone else's problem. Engage in active dialogue across your business, get customer insights now, and begin defining a future state and the key success factors you need to get there. Be the leader driving the data-driven marketing culture. This change can't be delegated. Define a vision and get the help you need to turn it into strategies for your business that drive more value.

Don't boil the ocean. Start with small steps and evolve. I've seen too many projects get sidelined by visions that are too big, coupled with steps that are too complex. Maintain a big and compelling vision, but identify low-hanging fruit for individual projects. For example, decide to increase revenue through better relationship marketing, and then identify the key initiatives that will deliver results.

Don't stagnate. Many projects in marketing are currently self-funded and, due to budget cuts and competing priorities, these initiatives often limp along. Complicating matters even more, it takes time to build credibility among the internal cynics needed to support certain projects. Put focus and resources behind strategic customer engagement projects. Then, staff these initiatives with people who can build relationships. You'll need to leverage expertise and manpower from all parts of the company (not just marketing) to create alignment and move forward.

2

Why Is Marketing Antiquated?

External forces, like the digital disruption I discussed in Chapter 1, aren't the only factors keeping marketers in the Dark Ages. When I talk to marketers one on one or speak with a roomful of business executives, I also hear about a wide range of internal obstacles that prevent companies from leveraging big data insights and developing more personal customer engagement strategies.

Though the details can vary widely, the most common challenges these organizations face include: a lack of collaboration across departments, mercurial market and consumer behaviors, turf wars over customer data ownership, ad hoc processes, declining or stagnant budgets, overspecialized functions, and proliferating channels. These problems are spun from years of ever-changing marketing leadership and a shift in buying practices caused by a variety of factors, most notably, the Internet, mobile devices, social networks, and a global marketplace that is now always on and constantly connected.

Why has marketing lost pace to these challenges? Because in many instances, marketers are unable to clear at least one (and usually more) of these six stubborn hurdles:

- Tactical (versus strategic) marketing
- Manual marketing management
- Silos of data and demand for real-time engagement
- Communicating the value of marketing
- Lack of talent/training
- Fragmented and often missing data

Let's discuss each of these hurdles so you can better understand why it's so difficult for marketing to emerge from the Dark Ages.

Tactical (versus Strategic) Marketing

In many firms, the marketing function is purely tactical. Often, business-to-business (B2B) marketers are focused on supporting sales with lead generation, internal slide development, and content creation for sales-enablement tools. In other companies, marketers are considered the "arts and crafts" department, and their main deliverables are websites and those tedious PowerPoint templates.

By contrast, in forward-thinking firms, a completely different dynamic has taken root. In these companies, the marketing function has evolved from tactical to *strategic*. Here, marketing drives the product and services roadmap, designs the buyers' journey, and essentially, directs the business. Of course, to take on this strategic role, marketers have to embrace an approach that uses data and insights to inform decisions. These firms recognize marketing as a new strategic opportunity and realize it's the foundation for the entire company's success.

Why? Because when marketers shift from tactical to strategic roles, they're empowered to become customer-centric. Guided by this new focus, they start charting the course to innovation and propelling the change that's necessary to compete in today's global marketplace.

As I mentioned earlier, marketers have always been the experts when it comes to understanding customers. The difference is that marketers can now use small and big data analytics to link the customer directly to company revenue. As a result, they can *prove* the value of their strategy and justify changes across the organization.

Manual Marketing Management

Unfortunately, most traditional go-to-market processes impede marketers from participating in high-level strategic planning. Think about it: Each quarter, marketers juggle hundreds of projects and thousands of creative and visual assets. They need a rich variety of content and a wide selection of offers and messages tailored to offline and online audiences. Managed manually, these initiatives devour the workday and leave little time for the strategic big picture. In short, too many marketers are still producing materials by hand using point solutions. Stuck in the Dark Ages, they still waste time scrolling through emails to manage the creative review process.

They still perform manual list uploads to segment and communicate with their target audience. Is it any wonder manual marketers like these are battling irrelevance?

And outdated content creation and review processes are only the tip of the iceberg. Marketing is one of the largest variable spends for most companies today. So I'm baffled that many organizations still manage their sizeable marketing budgets in basic spreadsheets. They don't link each campaign or initiative to its cost and results, and they're far from tracking or reconciling marketing spend to overall corporate financials or objectives. It would be absurd for a global corporation to use Excel workbooks to track its overall finances, so why was it ever considered acceptable for marketing? The pressure on chief marketing officers (CMOs)to prove the return on marketing investment (ROMI) has never been greater, so why is marketing the last frontier to integrate and automate its processes, systems, and data? The antiquated approach of manual project management keeps marketing in the Dark Ages and leaves its true value locked up on spreadsheets and hidden in fractured enterprise systems.

Traditionally, marketing has not been forced to tie its spend and results to overall business goals and metrics. A department that has long been excused from the demands for quantitative rigor, marketing now stands at an inflection point, and in order to move forward, marketers must begin managing the business of marketing. What do I mean by *the business of marketing*? Marketing oversees a large portfolio of assets, including financial and human resources, projects that span the business and geographies, and intellectual property through content and go-to-market strategies. Marketers need to manage these valuable assets with greater discipline and process to assure they are optimizing and driving revenue and competitive advantage at the lowest cost.

Silos of Data and Demand for Real-time Engagement

Consumers are in control. They're demanding real-time responses that are relevant and personalized, and available when, where, and how they want them. This dynamic is driving marketers to fix inherent process bottlenecks so their teams can react to consumers quickly and effectively. Beyond the technology to integrate information from different channels and customer touchpoints, marketers need the data and content to respond in real time.

Retailers are among the first to deal with this shift in control as the proliferation of mobile devices is revolutionizing the retail shopping experience. A 2012 Teradata study of more than 2,000 consumers[1] found that one in five consumers is now "showrooming," visiting retail stores to try products, then checking a mobile device for the best price online. Of those already showrooming, 33 percent said they ultimately used the information to buy elsewhere. And the trend is only expected to grow. Nearly everyone in the study (96 percent) said they plan to use their smart phone to research prices the same way or more in the future.

How can retailers combat the showrooming trend? As I see it, the brick-and-mortar retailers that succeed will be the ones that change the in-store dynamic. They'll use big data marketing insights to empower employees, so then these employees can treat shoppers they way they want to be treated: as individuals with unique buying behaviors and preferences. For instance, by using data-driven marketing, retailers can learn what each customer values most: whether that's a discount, bonus reward points, an extended warranty, or some other perk. Then, they'll be able to offer that preferred option to the shopper who's showrooming, right then and there, on the sales floor.

Granted, all of this is part of good, old-fashioned customer service—and that may be what today's consumers want most of all! In fact, 85 percent of consumers polled in the 2010 North American Customer Experience Report published by RightNow Technologies said they are willing to pay above the standard price of a product or service to ensure they receive a superior experience.[2]

Other industry sectors are feeling the effects of empowered consumers, too, and fortunately, most companies are not blind to this new consumer clout and the potential business impact of a poor customer experience. In particular, today's social media networks take word of mouth to a whole new level. Here's a case in point: Back in 2009, a disgruntled customer created a YouTube video to describe his bad experience with a well-known brand. The video went viral. More than 500,000 people viewed it in three days, and the bad press reportedly cost the brand $5 million in the first month. Bottom line: Consumers won't remain silent with the power and reach of the Internet and social networks literally at their fingertips—a conclusion verified by survey results released in April 2013. Dimensional

Research found that nearly six in ten of those surveyed (58 percent) said they are more likely to tell others about their customer service experiences today than they were five years ago.[3]

I find that when I poll CMOs and their senior leadership teams, their number-one strategic focus is to provide a more compelling customer experience. My advice is always the same: Focus on the external experience and work inward, improving customer information and data at each interaction point with the explicit goal of adding value for the individual and bolstering the trust that forms the foundation of customer relationships. Essentially, to improve the customer experience, you need to consolidate data, make sure your systems work together, and capture, collect, harmonize, and utilize information to enable more informed and timely engagement across all channels.

Communicating the Value of Marketing

Even when a company's processes are integrated, automated, collaborative, and strategic, there will be tension in the C-suite if employees cannot effectively demonstrate results. These days, there's a laser focus on accountability and transparency, and marketers are expected to deliver a higher degree of performance and metric-driven discipline than ever before. In response, marketing executives are learning to embrace a data-driven marketing culture. They're implementing new technologies to harness big data, integrate operations, and produce credible, tangible metrics. They're nurturing collaborative partnerships, and they're retraining or up-leveling talent to satisfy the demand for analytical skills in almost every modern marketing position.

Even so, communicating the value of marketing isn't always easy. Let me give you a personal example. I worked for nearly seven years at a multinational computer technology corporation in Silicon Valley, California. During my first year, I sat in research and development, where I led global CRM product marketing and frequently debated with senior leadership about how I believed marketing was more than clever words and pretty slide presentations. During this Dark Age of my own career, my colleagues kidded during staff meetings that they needed my "arts and craft" skills. They also jokingly told me to "get out the sock puppets" whenever I left to speak at external presentations. There is always a whisper of truth in humor, right? Without question, the C-suite at that organization viewed the marketing function as purely tactical—and back then, I didn't have the data I needed to prove my team's value. Now, I know better. Data, process, and content build credibility and demonstrate value . . . and value and revenue are what drive markets.

Lack of Talent and Training

Businesses can't move ahead into the Enlightened Age of Data if they don't leverage big data marketing—and they can't leverage big data marketing without the expertise of data scientists and others trained in skills like computational analysis, predictive modeling, statistics, and the management of big data sets. But, there's a problem: There just aren't enough data pros to fill all the needed positions, and that means opportunities are being lost while companies scramble to fill these crucial roles.

Teradata's most recent BARC Big Data Survey[4] found that most of the companies polled intend to invest in big data technologies; however, a lack of human resources and know-how keeps them from gaining deeper insights. In fact, insufficient technical and analytical expertise is the most imminent challenge when it comes to the use of big data.

The third State of Business Intelligence and Analytics survey echoed those results. In this survey, one-third of employer practitioners reported an overall lack of experience as their most important challenge, followed by insufficient business skills. Insufficient technical skills and a general lack of candidates tied for.[5] How are employers responding? The vast majority (80 percent) of employers surveyed offer supplemental training courses for newly hired workers, ranging from extensive classroom work to mentorship and internships to tuition reimbursement.

Fragmented and Often Missing Data

As you have undoubtedly realized by now, each one of the six hurdles outlined in this chapter is directly related to data. Yes, data holds enormous potential for business value. But, it can also present enormous roadblocks to progress. For example, when data is scattered in siloed systems—or incomplete, or missing, in general—customer relationship management

(CRM) applications fall short of expectations. They fail in their promise to create what many consider marketing's Holy Grail: the 360-degree view of the customer. In fact, most business executives I know laugh out loud when they hear that term because they know achieving that level of scope and specificity has been as elusive as finding Sasquatch, the Loch Ness Monster, or, of course, the Holy Grail. According to the *Global Teradata Data-Driven Marketing Survey, 2013*, only 18 percent of marketers routinely have a single view of all customer interactions.[6] Why so few?

The answer is simply that data fragmentation and data silos have created what I call a "data hairball," my term for the complicated mess of interactions, applications, information, and processes that now plagues a variety of different business functions. At some companies, the data hairball consists of customer information spread across marketing, finance, sales, and customer support departments. At others, it's a snarl of data from marketing service providers (MSPs) and information trapped in channels like separate eCommerce sites, undocumented call center conversations, and web activity that leaves partial data strung across the company and partners. Figure 2.1 illustrates why marketers lack the systems and data they need to work together. As you can see, it's really quite simple. Marketers working in the Dark Ages are frustrated by a fractured hodgepodge of technology and channels. In Chapter 3, I'll explain how this jumble impacts the customer.

CEOs, CMOs, and their teams now wrestle with data hairballs every day. They yearn to capture more insights and drive more relevant content and conversations, and yet, despite their best efforts, the tangles usually just grow bigger and more complex. The uncomfortable reality is that most current information management systems simply aren't up to the task. They can't handle large data sets and they can't perform advanced analytics. Then, as the number and variety of channels and applications continue to explode, these older systems simply fall farther and farther behind.

Sure, many marketers are talking about big data; but very few understand how to tackle it, and even fewer have begun to leverage it within their organizations to inform more strategic, value-based customer engagement strategies. As I'll reveal throughout this book, the true value of big data comes from insights, and those insights are only possible after the integration of data (both traditional and multi-structured) from different sources, such as digital, offline, internal, and external.

Are you ready to dig in deeper? Let's explore the relationship between marketing and data in more detail, starting with the next chapter.

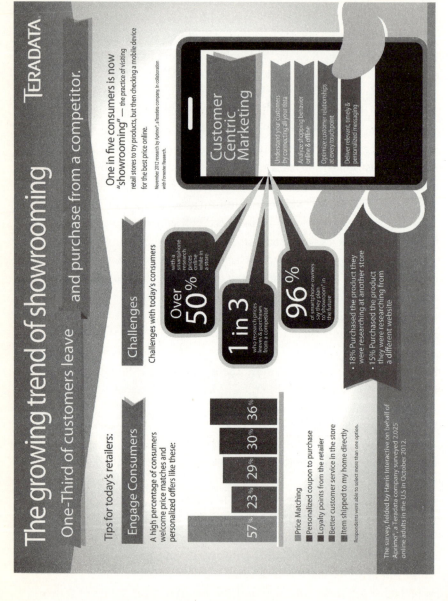

FIGURE 2.1 The Showrooming Trend

Source: © Teradata/Aprimo, 2012

KEY TERMS

Return on Marketing Investment (ROMI): A metric used to measure a marketing initiative's overall effectiveness and contribution to objectives like company revenue. Understanding ROMI helps marketers make better decisions about allocating future investments. This metric is a common language for marketers to communicate the value of their efforts to the rest of the organization. Chapter 9 provides more detail on this concept.

Data hairball: The complicated mess of interactions, applications, information, and processes that results when companies are unprepared to handle information from a wide range of data sources, many of which are not organized in an orderly manner, complicating usage and access.

Showrooming: The practice of visiting retail stores to try products, then checking a mobile device to find the best price online.

DOs AND DON'Ts

Recognize that traditional marketing technologies, processes, and culture need to evolve or risk becoming irrelevant. The modern marketing department must respond, often in real-time, to demands from the C-suite and a growing variety of stakeholders, including customers, collaborators, and vendors. Manual processes and a business-as-usual mindset can no longer keep pace.

Identify where and how your data is fragmented. Begin by appointing a data-savvy, process-driven individual to lead the charge. Map out where data is being generated and where there's influx from new digital channels. Then, build a project

(continued)

(*continued*)

plan for collecting and managing that data. Consider master data management technologies and a strong partnership with IT to make it happen.

Put the customer at the center of all you do. Today's empowered consumers expect personalized, relevant interactions. When was the last time you stood in your customers' shoes and saw what it was like to do business with your company and use your product or service? Take a day or two to experience your company as a customer. One airline refused to allow its leadership team to fly first class to ensure they would understand how the majority of passengers experience their services. Understand the customer journey and inspire your organization and others on how to revolutionize the customer experience.

Don't add unnecessary complexity to the marketing hairball. Plot your course. Create a data management plan to ensure your moves are meaningful. Don't stop collecting data simply because you aren't currently using it. Who knows? It could turn out to be an integral part of the next project to improve customer engagement. Just don't get ahead of yourself. Start small and build as your capabilities improve.

Don't bury your head in the sand. The data hairball may be overwhelming, and you may have a deficit of talent needed today to modernize marketing. Embrace the reality of where your team and data are today and commit to driving change and improving the picture.

Don't accept status quo. Your company might be growing, but if you believe your marketing approaches are outdated, do something about it. Digital disruption requires us to evaluate, execute, and evolve go-to-market strategies. What worked today won't always work tomorrow.

3

The Data Hairball

The relationship between marketing and data is one of the most challenging strategic opportunities facing companies today. In fact, I'll even go a step further. It shouldn't surprise you to learn that, as the chief marketing officer (CMO) of Teradata Applications, I consider this relationship to be *the* most challenging and exciting strategic opportunity facing companies today. Marketers have spent years struggling with data access and management, and they've grappled long and hard with how to apply data to drive better marketing and consumer engagement. But now, the wrestling match is getting even more difficult to win—thanks to digital disruption, our always on, always connected culture, and the fragmentation of information across multiple, varied channels. Make no mistake about it: The data dilemma is growing, and there's no end in sight.

How can marketers get their arms around these issues? Where's a good place to start? What's at the *heart* of the problem?

This may sound counterintuitive, but the actual core of the problem is that marketers *don't have* the data they need. But wait—didn't I say a moment ago in the previous chapter that marketers are waged in a battle against *too much* data? How can marketers have too much data, and yet not have the data they need? Well, you see, data *quantity* and data *quality* are two distinctly different things. Gathering digital inputs—whether by the terabyte, the petabyte, the exabyte, or more—does not equate with knowledge.

I like to sum it up like this: *More data does not equal the right data, and data alone does not equal insight.*

What Is the Data Hairball?

Yes, we are going to spend some time talking about hairballs—data hairballs to be exact. While I realize even the thought of a hairball probably evokes a visceral, unpleasant reaction for you, that's precisely my intention. You see, the feeling caused by thinking about a hairball is similar to what many CMOs feel whenever they think about the chaos of data surrounding marketing.

What is the data hairball? The data hairball is the biggest obstacle to improving customer engagement. It is the complicated mess of interactions, applications, data, and processes that accumulate unchecked when companies are unprepared to handle information from a wide range of sources. The data hairball embodies both the promise and the threat behind big data and digital channels.

Marketing, IT, sales, and others may all be working to collect data. But has your organization transcended systems and organizational lines to pull all of this information together? Probably not. According to the *Global Teradata Data-Driven Marketing Survey, 2013* I mentioned in Chapters 1 and 2, less than one-third of marketers own and control customer data. About half rely on IT for access to data.[1]

It's a given that business success now depends on your ability to collect and integrate digital information with traditional offline data, but your marketing strategies will always fall short if that's *all* you do. You must go a step further and leverage big data analytics to transform your data into actionable insights. As difficult as it may be for some to hear, the truth is, without using insights to adjust and optimize marketing activities, all efforts at aggregation and integration are largely wasted.

The Data Hairball and the Customer Experience

Take a minute to put yourself in your customers' shoes. I guarantee many of them are wondering why your company clogs their inboxes with emails every week, but doesn't know their preferences when they phone your call center. Sure, you've proven you can assist them by phone. You've shown them you can collect email addresses and pump out messages at predetermined intervals. But have you given your customers a holistic experience across these interaction channels? Does your call center, local storefront, or branch know the customer on the other side of the phone or counter? Have you determined how your customers interact with your messages? And if you answered no to at least one of those questions—as I suspect you did—why *don't* you know your customers better?

Here's my educated guess: Your data is fragmented. Your channels are fragmented. Your messages are fragmented. And as a result, the customer experience is fragmented, too. You don't know your customers better because you're caught up in the data hairball, and the hairball is choking the creation of compelling customer experiences. Figure 3.1 depicts a simplistic view of the customer experience across an enterprise. Imagine the impact it has on loyalty, and ultimately brand value.

How does your organization define *the customer experience*? I find that definitions of this term vary from company to company; most want to impart their own meaning to the phrase. To Harley Manning at Forrester, the customer experience is "how customers perceive their interactions with your company."[2] Colin Shaw, CEO of Beyond Philosophy who is often referred to as "The Customer Experience Guru," defines it as "an interaction between an organization and a customer as perceived through a customer's

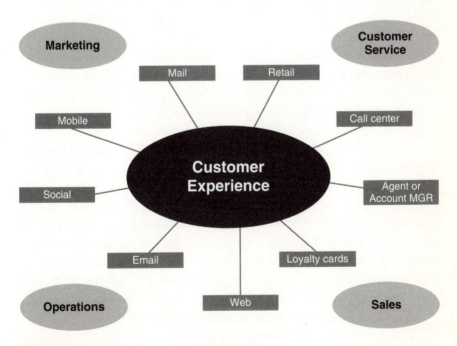

FIGURE 3.1 The Customer Experience

Source: © Teradata/Aprimo 2011

conscious and subconscious mind. It is a blend of an organization's rational performance, the senses stimulated and emotions evoked, and intuitively measured against customer expectations across all moments of contact."[3]

The definitions may vary, but one consistent thread runs through them all: The customer experience involves all interactions and touchpoints. So, as marketing channels continue to multiply, the customer experience becomes more and more complex. It's no wonder that in study after study, marketers cite complexity as one of the greatest barriers to improving multichannel customer engagement—and yet, the customer experience directly relates to business revenue growth.

Blending Art and Science

As I'll explore in more detail in the remaining chapters, companies need to use the imperative of improved customer engagement to start unraveling the hairball. That's the only way to acquire the insights necessary to innovate and deliver a more compelling customer experience, one that leads to competitive advantage.

There's no question that modern marketing technology is essential to drive sales. But keep in mind that technology by *itself* is not sufficient. These days, marketers must balance the science of numbers with the art of creativity to remain bold, innovative, and responsive to customer needs and wants. As you've undoubtedly heard before, it doesn't make any sense to spend time looking for the secret sauce or a silver bullet to ensure success. Why not? Because there are as many different winning customer experiences as there are companies and brands.

Here's an example to illustrate my point. I work at the Teradata office in Indianapolis, Indiana, a city that boasts an award-winning Bureau of Motor Vehicles. Despite all the accolades this organization receives, do I linger when I'm done renewing my driver's license, wishing I could stay there for a few more minutes? No, and no one else I know wants to, either. The goal of the Bureau of Motor Vehicles (BMV) is to create an experience that gets its customers, the general public, in and out in the most efficient manner. The BMV knows we don't want to stick around.

By contrast, consider the customer experience offered by International Speedway Corporation (ISC), the world's leading promoter of motor sports. As I discuss at length in Chapter 11, ISC has made a commitment to provide highly personalized pre- and post-race experiences for its fans. "If you're one of the four million fans sitting in the seats of an ISC grandstand this year, ISC wants you to feel like the experience was designed for you alone," explains Jim Cavedo, ISC's senior director of consumer marketing.[4]

Integrated Marketing, Really

I can't stress this enough: Once you start untangling the data hairball and using analytics to find insights, you can't stop there. You must take action on those insights and use them to: adjust campaigns; optimize marketing spend; improve your media mix; provide truly personalized, relevant offers for each individual customer; and so on. In order to take that next step, you'll need to revolutionize your approach to people, process, and technology as you integrate and automate the function of marketing. Many companies are turning to sophisticated integrated marketing management (IMM) technology to help them in this transformation. I'll discuss IMM in much more detail in Chapter 10, but for now, suffice it to say that IMM solutions allow organizations to scale and execute on the insights uncovered by big data analytics.

Just ask Peggy Dyer, the CMO for the American Red Cross, who is transforming the way this vital not-for-profit engages with donors across systems, departments, and channels. Dyer knew the American Red Cross needed to update its marketing processes, but from the onset she also realized there would be no value to implementing technology in a vacuum. So, before turning to technology, Dyer worked to understand the donor experience and what could be done to improve it. Then, her team determined what data issues were preventing the American Red Cross from executing on donor initiatives.

Dyer was also savvy about onboarding new talent. She knew her team needed a few heavy hitters who understood data and data-driven marketing, and who had *been there* and *done that* with regard to driving relevant customer experiences. As she hired and fine-tuned the marketing organization, she also crystallized her vision of what the American Red Cross donor experience should look like. It was only then that Dyer and her team mapped out a plan, a comprehensive strategy that included simplifying and unifying data, updating internal marketing systems, and improving interaction channels and go-to-market processes.

Clearly, Dyer understands that insights without action are useless, and to be able to scale action on the insights big data analytics uncovered, she realized the American Red Cross needed to integrate and automate its marketing technology. From early on, Dyer also recognized and communicated to her team that the integration of marketing and the value the American Red Cross is delivering to donors is a journey, and she continually reinforces execution with a long-range vision. Consequently, her team sees this journey as a marathon, not a sprint. While there are moments that they may yearn to call it quits, the team at the American Red Cross has staying power. They know IMM is going to revolutionize how they market and how they engage with their donors. Meanwhile, Dyer and her team continue to fuel the transformation by meeting with the senior marketing leadership team to discuss skill and talent development, big data, mobile, and social channels, so they can keep up with trends and continue to drive innovation and improve the donor experience.[5]

Data Privacy and Security

All this complexity, combined with the new ways to leverage data insights, also contributes to growing concerns about data privacy and security. Every time I speak to a roomful of marketers, I field questions about adapting to the world of big data. These marketers aren't only concerned about which data they *can* use; they're also concerned about which data they *should* use. They have questions about how they can ensure the data they collect will be secure. They want to know the best ways to build trust with customers, to make them feel comfortable sharing their data in the first place.

Let's be honest. In the past, marketers haven't exactly earned gold stars for their restraint and transparency. They've engaged in practices like robocalling, "spray and pray" email campaigns, and intrusive SMS advertising. A few years ago, there were even revelations of creepy geo-location tracking by companies like Google and Apple. Yes, marketers have sometimes pushed the envelope with customer data. So it's no surprise consumers have begun pushing back.

Here in the United States, the Direct Marketing Association (DMA) is leading the way to promote responsible data-driven marketing by maintaining and enforcing industry-standard guidelines for ethical marketing. These guidelines are based on not just what is legal, but what is the right thing to do for customers, and the 10 DMA Member Principles reflect them, assuring consumers that DMA member organizations will use customer information in a manner that respects the customers' wishes. As consumers, our modern lifestyles are so enabled by marketing data that we hardly notice it's there. Everything from product reviews and recommendations to geo-located offers to real-time, cross-channel shopping carts to advertising banners are tailored to our interests. Perhaps because these advantages are so ingrained in our daily lives, public policy makers and regulators have started to notice the prevalence of marketing data. DMA CEO Linda Woolley calls on marketers to help DMA educate policy decision makers on how marketers add value to consumers and the economy, and DMA is always seeking examples of how data used for marketing purposes will help counter misunderstandings about what marketers do. As Woolley explains, "It's up to us to act responsibly, put customers first, and clearly demonstrate how using marketing data helps drive value without compromising individuals' privacy."[6]

Europe has experienced its own wave of sweeping e-privacy directives. These require all marketers and website owners operating in any EU country to obtain consent from European users before implementing cookies or other technologies to capture online visitor information. As I'm sure you're aware, digital marketers routinely use cookies and other technologies to tailor online customer experiences, enable web analytics, recommend products, allow auto-log in, and compile browsing histories. Essentially, the EU's e-privacy directives mean cookies can only be placed on machines where a user or subscriber has opted-in (as many consumers do so they can benefit from a more personalized online experience).

Other new consumer privacy movements are germinating in Europe, as well. For instance, some are advocating for the "right to be forgotten," which would give individuals the power to clear their past digital behavior from company and network logs. The proposal, which many fear could obliterate our online footprints and lead to tremendous confusion and frustration, continues to get press both in Europe and the United States.

How do rules like this apply to your marketing strategies? To help marketers and business owners better understand the EU regulations, the UK's Information Commissioner's Office (ICO) created a website (www.ico.gov.uk/) that offers guidance on use of cookies and similar technologies. I advise all marketers to look to the ICO and the EU in general, as Europe is emerging as the pioneer regarding consumer privacy in our digital world.

In addition, it's also worth pointing out that even though legislation is emerging as a means to answer tricky questions about how companies manage consumer data, many leading marketing academics feel government regulation is not the ideal solution. For instance, Professor John Deighton of Harvard Business School suggests a different way. "The information age needs to rest on something more robust than regulation. . . . the secure foundation for the new go-to-market regime is institutional, not rule-based. What kind of institution? One that pays consumers for their data in money or in positive experiences by creating for them a valued identity."[7]

As Deighton explains, consumers are in control; they have the power to share their data or not. It's up to companies, therefore, to make sharing that data worthwhile.

"Consumers can achieve anonymity today by declining to join supermarket frequent shopper programs, but by so doing the average household pays $200 a year more for products," he writes. "The points awarded by airline frequent flyer and hotel frequent guest programs, if redeemed, amount to discounts of 1 percent to 5 percent over the prices paid by non-subscribers. They also lose out on a variety of non-monetary benefits like recognition and preferential service that may matter more than money."

Of course, it all boils down to trust between the buyer and the seller.

"I want Amazon to know my identity, in particular my taste in books and music," Deighton concludes. "I know that they respect the value of that knowledge so that the issue of sharing the data won't ever come up."

KEY TERMS

Customer experience: Every company has its own definition. I like to think of the customer experience as the sum of digital and physical interactions across an entire enterprise, and the emotional response the engagement triggers.

DOs AND DON'Ts

Integrate and automate your marketing point solutions, including email, campaign management, real-time interaction, and offer management, spend management, and analytics. An integrated marketing technology platform will help streamline your systems and help unify your customer data—a key step to unraveling the data hairball. You need a holistic and integrated approach so you can use marketing technology to fully leverage big data.

Create a customer experience that's unique to your brand. Be genuine. Be authentic. Respond to *your* customers' wants and needs. Keep track of innovations by other companies, but don't try to use every new engagement technique you see. Before you commit time and money to try a new tactic, analyze how your customers will experience it and whether your customers feel the interaction provides them something of value.

Use big data insights to elevate the customer experience. Compile, integrate, and analyze data across all touchpoints.

Don't focus solely on gathering more and more (and more) data. Data aggregation is only part of the solution; you also need big data analytics to help you find the actionable insights that are hidden in all that data. Integrated marketing solutions can help you automate how you leverage big data insights to optimize all aspects of your marketing and customer experience.

Don't be creepy. Studies have consistently shown that consumers are open to targeted marketing if they have **opted-in** and if the content is **relevant**. On the other hand, customers abandon businesses they perceive as dishonest or overly intrusive. Ask customers to opt-in, and then build relationships with them by providing goods, information, offers, or services of

(continued)

(continued)

value. Get to know your customers' likes and dislikes, and fine-tune your messages to be personalized and relevant for each individual.

Don't use technology in a vacuum. Rather, use it in combination with strategic plans, interdepartmental collaboration, and innovative thinking. Leverage technology to transform how you listen, analyze, and engage with customers and prospects. Blend the science of numbers with the art of creativity to innovate and elevate the customer experience.

Get Ready
for Big Data
Marketing

4

Definitions for the Real World of Big Data Marketing

One of my favorite films is 1967's *The Graduate*, which stars Dustin Hoffman as Benjamin Braddock, a 21-year-old who's confused about his future. It's summertime in the late 1960s and, in one of the movie's classic scenes, Mr. McGuire, a family friend, offers Benjamin career advice.

"I just want to say one word to you. Just one word," Mr. McGuire says.

"Yes, sir," Benjamin replies.

"Are you listening?" Mr. McGuire asks.

"Yes, I am."

Mr. McGuire pauses, and then, as if he's letting Benjamin in on one of the best-kept secrets of all time, he says the one word "*Plastics.*"

Now, plastics may have been the hot business tip back in 1967, but times have changed. If someone remade *The Graduate* today, Mr. McGuire would offer a different one-word nugget. I have no doubt he'd tell Benjamin to pursue—"Are you listening?"—*data.*

Data. Virtually every time we use technology in today's digitized world, whether it's to communicate, shop, learn, relax, or interact, we leave a trail of digital information behind us. That's all data, and as it accumulates over time, across devices and web properties, it becomes *big data*. It develops into a reflection of how we spend our time, what is important to us, what we like, and even what we want. Combine all these external digital inputs with the financial, marketing, service, and demographic information already trapped within your enterprise, and you get *really* big data.

Once marketers are able to unlock and harness big data, it can pave the path to the so-called marketing Holy Grail, that elusive 360-degree view of the customer. Data drives better insights, and those insights drive better interactions—allowing you to truly deliver the right message over the right channel at the right time to the right customer. In turn, these enhanced interactions result in increased revenue and competitive differentiation.

Let me give you and example of a brand that has used better data to improve the way they interact with consumers.

For decades, Shop Direct Group, a UK retail group that includes brands like Very.co.uk, Littlewoods, and isme, managed enormous volumes of data on customer catalog transactions, all of which provided rich insights into preferences. However, with the emergence and proliferation of online commerce, Shop Direct lacked the capabilities to connect customer experience data across all channels, including its call center, website, and catalog. The company needed to both manage this data complexity, and obtain more accurate and timely information about its customers, specifically, their sentiments and buying intentions.

Shop Direct developed a strategy and a technology roadmap to meet the data challenge head on. The company consolidated its data across multiple offline and online channels in a data warehouse complemented with digital tagging solutions that can capture and share customer interaction behavior across multiple channels. Those behavioral insights support highly relevant and personalized messages.

"We wanted to understand our customers' true intentions so we used technology to store cross-channel data and perform analytics, and saw a 20 percent increase in conversion rates for abandoned basket and browsers; 28 percent incremental uplift with each email sent; a 10 percent reduction in direct marketing costs; and a 50 percent decrease in printed catalogues," a spokesperson from the company reported.[1]

More and more marketers are realizing what those at Shop Direct Group now know. They're motivated to offer an improved overall brand experience, and they know data-driven marketing technologies are essential to make it happen. The *Global Teradata Data-Driven Marketing Survey, 2013* found that 78 percent of marketers now are under pressure to become more data-driven. But, there's a hitch: Despite recognizing the need for these new capabilities, only 35 percent said their marketing organization had a data-driven strategy.

Those results echo what I hear when I meet with chief marketing officers (CMOs). Whether they're from a Fortune 50 or a global growing enterprise, most marketing executives admit they don't have the data—or more precisely, they don't have the data *insights*—they need to bring change to their companies and improve interactions with consumers. They also realize they need to remedy these deficits immediately. That's why I wasn't surprised when I heard Gartner analyst Laura McLellan predict that by 2017, CMOs will spend more on IT than their counterpart, chief information officers (CIOs).[2]

Chief *marketing* officers will soon be spending more on IT than chief *information* officers. Why? Because marketing is becoming increasingly technology-based, and harnessing and mastering big data is now absolutely necessary for achieving competitive advantage. Plus, don't forget that many marketing budgets are already larger—and faster growing—than IT budgets.

Clearly, marketing organizations across the globe are striving to become more data-driven, and CMOs are beginning to grapple with the reality that they will need to step up to improve data-driven capabilities across the entire enterprise, as well. After all, the data hairball I discussed in Chapter 3 is enormously complex and unwieldy. It could never be contained neatly within only the marketing department. It extends from marketing and ensnares multiple enterprise functions, including customer service, finance, and others. There's no doubt a cross-team focus will be required to sort through the mess.

At first, untangling the hairball may seem like a daunting task; however, marketers have no choice but to rise to the challenge. Waiting will only delay the inevitable and make it even more difficult to unravel the confusion. Tackling it now will help you learn what you don't know and inspire you to take steps to resolve any problems. Best of all, you can use the data insights you gather at each step along the way to improve your customer engagement strategies; that way, you'll immediately add more value to both your offline and online interactions.

The best way for CMOs and their teams to start is by cleaning their own houses first, so before we undertake the data hairball issue, let's step back and carefully consider the language we're using. Are you sure everyone in your organization knows exactly what you mean when you use terms like *big data* or *digital messaging* or *data-driven marketing*? Is everyone on your team on the same page? Are they even using the same playbook? Do yourself a favor and take the time to align organizations and people behind common definitions of the terms shaping the Enlightened Age of Data. While this may sound elementary, you'd be surprised how many cross-functional initiatives define goals, project timelines, and key deliverables, but fail to align on nomenclature and definitions. A best practice in the world of data-driven marketing is for the change agents, the leaders, to align across the organization and confirm that everyone shares an understanding of the terms used and the intent of any initiative related to those terms. They need to create a common language to facilitate change and help avoid the organizational "drag" produced by confusion, misunderstandings, and even hidden agendas.

While each enterprise needs to determine its own individual way to define these terms, I use the following definitions to describe the data-driven marketing landscape:

Big Data Terminology

Big data is a collection of data from traditional and digital sources that represents a source for ongoing discovery and analysis. I've run across definitions that constrain big data to digital inputs like web behavior and social network interactions; however, the CMOs and CIOs I talk with agree that we can't exclude traditional data derived from product transaction information, financial records, and interaction channels, such as the call center and point-of-sale. All of that is big data, too, even though it may be dwarfed by the volume of digital data that's growing at an exponential rate. In defining big data, it's also important to understand the mix of unstructured and multi-structured data that comprises the volume of information.

Unstructured data comes from information that is not organized or easily interpreted by traditional databases or data models, and typically, it's text-heavy. Metadata, Twitter tweets, and other social media posts are good examples of unstructured data.

The term multi-structured data refers to a variety of data formats and types and can be derived from interactions between people and machines, such as web applications or social networks. A great example is web log data, which includes a combination of text and visual images along with structured data like form or transactional information. As digital disruption transforms communication and interaction channels—and as marketers enhance the customer experience across devices, web properties, face-to-face interactions, and social platforms—multi-structured data will continue to evolve.

As I mentioned in Chapter 1, industry leaders like the global analyst firm Gartner use phrases like "volume, velocity, and variety" to frame the big data discussion.[3] I've also seen two other V's added: *veracity* and *value*.

For this book and the business audience, let's stick to the three V's: volume, velocity, and variety.

What exactly do those terms mean?

Volume

Volume is the amount of data, and it includes data from traditional and non-traditional sources. Think about the transactional data from a typical grocery store shopper—the products purchased, the frequency of each sale—that's all big data. Now couple that traditional data with the digital data from that shopper's Facebook page. Then, add all other shoppers' Facebook pages, too. As remarkable as it sounds, there is now the equivalent of 100 terabytes of data uploaded to Facebook every day.[4] How big is that? To give you a frame of reference, 100 terabytes is equivalent to the space to store 33 million songs. That's the volume of data uploaded to Facebook every day . . . and that's just one social platform.

Velocity

Velocity is the speed of information generated and flowing into the enterprise. Numerous analysts have tried to explain the mind-boggling exponential growth of data. According to the International Data Corporation (IDC), there will be 40 zettabytes of data generated annually by 2020. With 2.8 zettabytes generated in 2012, this means the digital universe will about double every two years until 2020.[5]

Variety

Variety is the kind of data available to companies and their marketing teams: sensor data, SMS data, web clickstream data. The list of data types is long, and it will continue to grow, adding to the complexity of the data hairball. Keep in mind: Marketing is both the end-user and a generator of big data. Given that the *Global Teradata Data-Driven Marketing Survey, 2013* found that only 18 percent of marketers have a single view of their target audience, we certainly have our work cut out for us as we work to improve and optimize Big Data Marketing opportunities.

Big Data Marketing

Also known as data-driven marketing, big data marketing is the process of collecting, analyzing, and executing on the insights you've derived from big data to encourage customer engagement, improve marketing results, and measure internal accountability. As I explained above, big data is structured and unstructured data spawned by traditional and digital channels. You need to combine all of this information with enterprise data so that marketing—and the entire company—can utilize it most effectively.

Integrated Marketing Management (IMM)

IMM is the process of merging and streamlining internal and external marketing functions, including data, processes, people, channels, and technologies.

Marketing Operations Management

Big data marketing relies on a set of processes and applications that provide a framework to systematically plan, manage, and execute marketing operations, including budget, marketing planning, and content management. This comprehensive program is marketing operations management.

Customer Interaction Management

Managing customer information across multiple touchpoints, including the Internet, mobile, social media, and offline channels, is crucial for marketing success. By harnessing advanced analytics and marketing communication features, customer interaction management provides more relevant conversations with customers, which, in turn, lead to more profitable, satisfying, and long-lasting relationships. Customer interaction management evolved from campaign management, and includes expanded analytical and digital engagement capabilities.

Digital Messaging

Digital messaging includes any of a variety of tech-based marketing communications, including email, SMS messages (texting), mobile app notifications, and social media posts.

Digital Marketing

While many of us understand the fundamental concept of digital marketing, it is important we are truly talking about the same thing when we use the term. Adam Sarner, a vice president and 15-year veteran at Gartner, researches, analyzes, and advises global brands on social customer relationship management (CRM) and customer engagement. He describes digital marketing as a tech-based, two-way marketing approach that acts as a decision tool involving and anticipating customers' wants and needs.[6] A great example of digital marketing is when a consumer visits a website, clicks on a product, abandons it, and then sees that same product appear as an advertisement on his Facebook page. Other examples involve value-added content versus straight-up advertisements; with these, the consumer and the marketer share more interactions.

DOs AND DON'Ts

Define the terms above for your own organization. Be certain you have alignment on your definitions, and that these terms work within your company. Then, make sure everyone on your team understands the language you are using.

Ask questions. Big data marketing represents new territory for many marketers, and it's okay not to have all the answers. Welcome dialogue to seek a deeper understanding and help teams understand there are no dumb questions in the Enlightened Age of Data.

Find talent to help drive the integration and collection of data. Hire, retrain, or up-level employees to satisfy the changing requirements of various marketing roles. In addition, nurture collaborations and implement new technology to harness big data, integrate operations, and produce credible, tangible metrics.

Don't wait. Many businesses will continue to wait for perfect conditions before they tackle the big data issue. Procrastination is dangerous, though, especially if your market is fierce, and

(continued)

(*continued*)

your competition is already making the necessary adjustments. Identify the right person to lead, and begin *today*.

Don't be afraid to fail. You don't know what you don't know, so the sooner you begin the process, the sooner you'll know what's required for success. Don't be afraid to set goals and then adjust. The only way to truly fail here is to fail to get started!

5 Meet the Modern Marketing Department (Michelangelo Meets Einstein)

Marketers take heart. Despite all the changes happening throughout the industry, chief marketing officer (CMO) tenure is on the rise. Thank goodness! Back in 2006, CMOs had a super-short shelf-life, averaging only 23 months.[1] Granted, I helped fuel that trend in some of my past CMO gigs, as they seemed to run only 14–24 months, depending on my resolve—or the company's. But, that was then, and this is now, and yes, I'm pleased to report that CMOs are sticky, once again.

I've enjoyed my current CMO role for nearly four years, a record among my multiple tries in this executive position. In the past, I was a traditional brand CMO. I helped revamp brand positioning by establishing foundational growth strategies to stimulate revenue and market share leadership. But more often than not, I lacked the insights and data to be sufficiently data-driven. As a result, I failed to grow beyond the brand role to where my colleagues, managers, and clients could see me as a true revenue contributor for my companies. I struggled to effectively educate my colleagues about the new and broader mission that was emerging for marketing, and I had trouble earning the credibility to make that broader change a reality.

Fortunately, at Aprimo (the integrated marketing management software firm that became Teradata Applications after its acquisition in early 2011), I managed to flip my old paradigm on its head. When I joined the company in 2009, the marketing applications category was quickly growing, and we needed to transition from our positioning as a technology-based brand to a value-based solution. My first step was to make sure I understood the challenge at hand, so I began collecting data immediately upon starting my current role.

As part of my onboarding, I personally interviewed more than 40 key internal and external stakeholders to gather qualitative data and insights on the company, brand, solutions, and positioning. Then, I worked with Chicago-based strategic agency Mobium to meld the company's data-driven brand processes (both quantitative and qualitative) with mine to ensure we didn't outsource the insights and conviction needed to drive the change in brand positioning. I gathered data on our market, the buyer's journey, and the important buying criteria in the purchase decision. I considered our strengths, weaknesses, opportunities, and threats, so I could learn where to expand on what we could own. Ultimately, I combined all of this external data along with the internal stakeholder input I'd gathered, and used it to establish collaborative workshops with a cross-functional group of our leaders from research and development (R&D), sales, customer service, and our executive team. In these workshops, we worked to get alignment and buy-in across the company's leadership, and we began to define the brand and reinvigorate the market around a unique position at the time: integrated marketing management (IMM).

I heard time and again during those early days that our marketing organization was known only as a lead-generating organization, tasked and focused on setting the table for sales with qualified prospects who were likely to buy software. While that may not sound strange to business-to-consumer (B2C) marketers, many senior business-to-business (B2B) marketing leaders will understand why I found this so troubling. If our marketing organization were relegated to only generating leads, we'd be focused almost entirely on enabling a *sales-driven* organization. That kind of approach would drastically downplay the other business functions that marketing can drive and influence. It also meant the company would stay sales-driven, as opposed to becoming a truly *market-driven* organization where marketing and sales would work together.

As Lori Wizdo, Principal Analyst at Forrester, wrote in a 2012 blog, "Marketing now owns a much bigger piece of the lead-to-revenue cycle. And B2B marketers must take responsibility for engaging with the customer through most of the buying cycle."[2] The evolution to a market-driven organization was critical for Aprimo, especially given changes in the buying process that enable prospective customers to dictate their experiences. I knew from my conversations with the executive leadership team that they, too, wanted—and needed—marketing to have a more strategic role. Think about it: We are a company that *sells marketing software* to *marketers*. If anyone needed to be drinking their own champagne, it was us!

After hearing the good, the bad, and the ugly about the state of our marketing, my next focus was to align the team to drive growth. At that time, the company was on the rise at better than 30 percent a year in a growth market. Using corporate objectives, revenue growth, customer retention, and market leadership, we outlined a simple marketing scorecard. We aligned it with the company's goals, while also using it to broaden marketing's charter and measure our contribution to the business. (We'd been doing the work. Wasn't it time we started getting credit for it?)

Our new scorecard had five key measures we could use as metrics to evaluate the team:

1. **Demand generation** to measure marketing-generated pipeline leads and conversions to customers.
2. **Customer satisfaction**, which we would measure using Net Promoter Score (NPS) and another metric to reference health within our customer base.
3. **Sales productivity**, quantified by measuring and monitoring pipeline conversions.
4. **Brand awareness and market leadership** metrics, which we'd benchmark against our transformational and social voice (a measure of whether or not we were winning the market).
5. **Marketing effectiveness**, which we based on measuring cost per lead, return on marketing investment, and the health of the other four metrics. We developed this *übermetric* to help us see if we were moving the needle significantly enough. Over time, it became the true showcase of our software and the leanest, meanest return on marketing investment.

Although Teradata is a B2B company, and our metrics may not be the same key performance measures for all companies, I'm happy to see more and more CMOs working with similar strategic visions. Like me, they're striving to broaden and define their organizations' contributions—and they're beginning to better understand how metrics and analytics can help. Today's modern marketing departments are effective only when they listen to their customers and internal stakeholders and clearly define their missions and contributions. Then, they must measure and communicate those missions and contributions while executing a more compelling customer experience.

The CMO as a Change Agent

Sadly, redefining the role of marketing remains a long, laborious slog for many CMOs. Their departments are still mired in the Dark Ages. Some lack the skills, training, and/or financial resources to move forward. For others, the problem seems to be paralysis. After all, most people don't like change. It seems change always has been and always will be associated with anxiety. Throw in the latest hype about whatever new social media platform is poised to rock your world or a benchmark study that implies the competition is sprinting ahead, and it's easy to understand how fear can keep entire organizations frozen in place.

In his book *Linchpin: Are You Indispensable?*, author and marketing expert Seth Godin explains the evolutionary underpinnings of this fear. He describes the lizard brain, the little and ancient portion of our highly developed gray matter that is hard-wired to take over whenever we sense danger or threat. Our lizard brain is what prevents us from challenging convention in business. It makes us run away from failure, rather than embrace and learn from it. It keeps us trapped in the status quo.[3]

Clearing these stubborn emotional hurdles or bypassing our lizard brains is an important first step in the transformation process. At some point, every marketer must come to terms with the fact that there is no turning back. Survival today depends on accepting change—and success tomorrow will depend on driving change. We've reached a point where the marketplace demands a new breed of marketing innovator, someone who's both tech-savvy and a true business leader. But, please don't misunderstand: No one expects these new marketers to have all the answers. Instead, we need them to envision a different world, both internally and externally, for their teams, their companies, and their customers.

During a conference in 2011, I heard a marketing executive from FedEx say, "Our job as CMOs is to make the rest of the organization uncomfortable." That quickly became one of my favorite quotes. Yet, for many of us, "making the rest of the organization uncomfortable" runs counter to keeping our jobs and garnering coveted recognition as a team player. As brothers Chip and Dan Heath explain in *Switch: How to Change Things When Change Is Hard*, change is the result of leadership and tough calls, but our job as leaders is to appeal to our teams' emotions while we guide them on the path to that change. As change agents, CMOs can't merely paint the vision. They must inspire their teams to deliver on that vision, too.[4]

It is also imperative that we establish a culture of trust—and a culture that accepts a measure of failure. Jeffrey Hayzlett, former CMO of Kodak, talks candidly about the topic of failure whenever he works with CMOs. He encourages failure because without it, innovation and fresh thinking are nearly impossible to cultivate. Hayzlett's mantra is "no one is going to die" if there is a mistake made or a failed program. I agree. Nurturing a creative, fail-safe environment is a priority for me, and I coach my team to *execute, evaluate, and evolve* using an iterative process to test their ideas.

Successful companies are headed toward a different world, the Enlightened Age of Data, where traditional brand CMOs and other one-dimensional marketing professionals will struggle to keep a foothold. By contrast, *renaissance* CMOs know they need help to solve issues posed by big data, process, and technology, and they address these challenges by adding fresh talent and new roles to their teams. Have you noticed an uptick in positions like vice president of CRM, marketing technology, or marketing operations? The titles may vary from company to company, but the gist is the same: The people in these new roles are the ones who will help untangle the big data hairball. They are collaborators who will help their organizations find the actionable insights required to elevate the customer experience and drive business growth.

The Data Scientist

I'm sure you've detected the common thread to all these new and re-configured roles: They all center on data and technology. Given Gartner's prediction that by 2017 CMOs will be spending more on technology than their counterpart chief information officers (CIOs), is it any wonder? It's also little surprise that we're seeing organizations scramble to find and hire experts who specialize in these fields. Often referred to as data scientists, these new business leaders understand that today, data drives revenue. They're trained in subjects like statistics and advanced predictive analytics, and they have experience working with big data sets.

The data scientist is a newer business role, and not every company is lucky enough to have one on board. But just because you haven't worked with one yet, don't make the mistake of thinking data scientists are unicorns, magical creatures that don't exist; nor are they unapproachable IT pros who don white lab coats and work in some ivory tower with their fellow geniuses. In fact, they're just the opposite. Data scientists are team members who can work collaboratively across the enterprise, and according to the *Harvard Business Review*, they have "the sexiest job in the 21st century."[5]

Perhaps Geoff Guerdat, Data Scientist for Gilt Groupe, the online flash-sale retailer, describes the role best. "It's integrating the data, but it's also using it, developing models, drawing relationships between things other people might not have seen," he says. "It's more than just integration; it's actually pattern recognition and data mining."[6]

Data scientists are leaders who help marketers combine the art of creativity with the science of numbers to drive insight and business results. They understand that marketing operations are strategic, and their job is to determine the qualitative expression of quantitative insights.

The CMO and CIO Dynamic

Back in 2005, when I was the CMO of Akamai, I talked to Christine Heckert, who was the CMO of Juniper Networks, about the growing need for collaboration between the CMO and CIO. In fact, Heckert had made the CMO-CIO relationship a priority at Juniper because she realized the business value of the peer-to-peer partnership. Looking back on that conversation from years ago, I'm disappointed that as of 2013, the relationship between IT and marketing hasn't materially improved for most companies. How can that possibly be? We know that customer experience and interactions are the focus in this age of digital disruption. We know that marketing is at the center of helping improve and drive an innovative engagement strategy. And we know that technology is the way we express most business strategy today. It only follows that the CIO and CMO need to be working together, driving change to drive business value.

Fortunately, some companies are beginning to tackle this issue, and a handful of different models are emerging. Currently, I see four distinct alternatives:

1. Unifying CIO and CMO roles
2. The emergence of a chief marketing technologist
3. The dawn of the chief digital officer
4. Collaboration with the chief customer experience officer

Unifying CIO and CMO Roles

Marketing is now a fundamental driver of IT purchasing, and that trend shows no signs of stopping or even slowing down any time soon.

As I mentioned, we all know marketing is becoming increasingly technology-based, and that harnessing and mastering big data is now key to achieving competitive advantage. In addition, many marketing budgets already are larger and faster growing than IT budgets. So, maybe the CMO and the CIO should be one in the same?

At Teradata, the CIO and the CMO are now unified under one senior-level leader, Bob Fair. The change is still relatively new, but the intent is to drive a consolidated vision and organization as we continue to evolve our customer and go-to-market experiences. The former CMO of Hyatt, Tom O'Toole, wore both hats from 2006 to 2008, as well. As Hyatt's chief marketing information officer, O'Toole drove the organization to accelerate and innovate its customer experience. He left Hyatt in 2010 to join United Airlines where he currently is the senior vice president of marketing and loyalty programs.

As always, culture and business objectives direct optimal organizational models. You'll need to carefully weigh whether unifying the CMO and CIO functions would accelerate or distract customer interaction innovation.

The Emergence of a Chief Marketing Technologist

At a Direct Marketing Association (DMA) conference, Tim McGuire, a principal at McKinsey and head of the Consumer Marketing Analytics Center, moderated a 2012 panel that explored how to bring marketing and IT together. In a blog post from December 2012, McGuire wrote about the conference and panel[7]:

> It was great to hear people talking about a range of experiences, from one end of the spectrum, where IT and marketers aren't communicating with each other, to the other end where they both are creating real value. But I was struck by the idea that what companies really need is a new role, such as a Chief Marketing Technology Officer. That's an idea we've heard before, but the need became very clear through the discussion as the panel focusing on the idea of a "bridge" to connect

marketing and technology and work in both environments. There can't be a fence between the two organizations, but it's not enough to tear those fences down. Organizations need to build bridges based on people with the talent to operate in both marketing and technology environments.

I must admit, I think the idea of a chief marketing technologist is a good one. Companies still need strong and focused breadth and story-telling behind their brands, *and* they also need to accelerate evolving and elevating the customer experience. A chief marketing technologist could partner with a CMO to help marketing express and execute strategies, bridge the divide with IT, and achieve competitive differentiation using technology.

One word of caution: If not linked closely with marketing, a chief marketing technologist could represent another silo, and the position may be best filled by a chief customer experience officer, or someone else, who worked closely with and fully understands the customer experience across all channels. In the end, CEOs and the entire C-suite will need to step back, think big, and build the organization they need to capitalize on today's disruptive trends.

The Dawn of the Chief Digital Officer

Given the growing importance of the digital experience and the expertise needed to understand the geeky side of digital marketing—digital marketing attribution, tags, dynamic digital profiles, and so on—companies are testing a new position in the C-suite, the chief digital officer (CDO). These digital gurus understand how to harness data behind social networks, web clicks, and conversions, and use it to drive a transformation digital strategy.

These strategic, digital savvy, and business-driven leaders have what it takes to help transform traditional businesses into digitally driven companies. Figure 5.1 illustrates the broad skill set today's CDO demonstrates in our digital world. William Rand, director of the Center for Complexity in Business at the University of Maryland's Robert H. Smith School of Business, describes the role in a 2012 article. "The goal of a CDO is to examine how digital technology can simplify and improve all business operations," he told *Teradata Magazine* online in an interview. "A good [CDO] should not just impact a single particular area, but impact every element of a

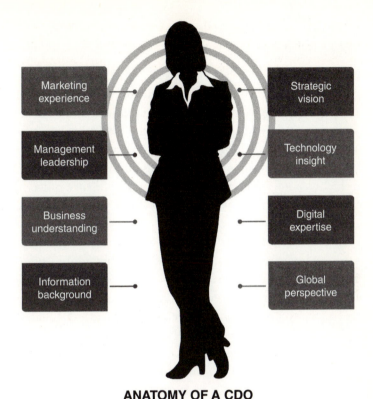

ANATOMY OF A CDO

Chief digital officers possess business acumen and technical expertise.

FIGURE 5.1   Anatomy of a CDO

Source: Teradata Magazine, "Digital Destiny," Q3 2012

business. For instance, a CDO might suggest an integrated platform that marketing, sales, and logistics can all use to trace advertising efforts, sales, and product movement, rather than having three separate systems."[8]

Where does this position best fit? For some companies, the chief digital officer reports directly to the CEO to drive enterprise-wide change. In others, the position reports to the CMO, yet carries the broad enterprise mission. Either way, Rand stresses that the relationship between the CDO and the CMO has to be a two-way street. According to an article by Robert Berkman entitled the "The Emergence of Chief Digital Officers," media-based businesses appear to be particularly enthusiastic about this role, which makes sense, given their growing dependence on digital business models.[9]

Collaboration with the Chief Customer Experience Officers

Another organizational alternative is to drive a more matrix-based approach with hardline and dotted-line reporting structures unifying formerly disparate teams. For example, in some companies, IT resources and customer insights departments are now distributed within marketing and other business functions, and they report back to a cross-enterprise team that sits in operations or finance. Eventually, these teams may report to emerging roles like the chief customer officer or the customer experience officer. In fact, one could imagine scenarios where the CMO reports to these executives, as well.

Companies are creating chief customer officers or customer experience officers to focus on the external buyer and work across the enterprise to drive the overall customer experience with a brand's products and services. These new C-suiters are charged with connecting the dots between the customer and the company, and to succeed, they must work collaboratively to align resources and execute against the broader plan.

The position of the customer experience officer has been embraced by a few firms, including the The Washington Post Company, a leading U.S. media outlet, and Merck, a large multinational pharmaceutical company. It appears that more organizations are embracing the chief customer officer position, with companies like Pacific Gas & Electric, MetLife, and Teradata leading the way.

All modern marketing departments share a common foundation; they are grounded in technology, customer experience, and data. Regardless of new titles, these teams have expanded their skill sets and become more externally focused as they apply data and technology to drive growth and value. As a result, modern marketing departments are vibrant and exciting, and the marketers there radiate a new level of confidence, now that processes are data-driven.

Is your organization ready for big data marketing? Is it time for you to move out of the Dark Ages and into the Enlightened Age of Data? Here are five steps, illustrated in Figure 5.2, to help guide you on your journey:

1. Get smart, get strategic.
2. Tear down the silos.
3. Untangle the data hairball.
4. Make metrics your mantra.
5. Process is the new black.

FIGURE 5.2 Five Marketing Steps

Source: © Teradata 2013

Over the next five chapters, I'll explore each step illustrated in Figure 5.2 in more detail, including case studies and thought leadership, to help you visualize and understand the opportunities at hand.

KEY TERMS

Change: To become different; to transform. But remember to strive for meaningful change. As Jeffrey Hayzlett says, "Change for change's sake is bad. The objective should be growth."[10]

(continued)

(continued)

Data scientist: The individual whose role is to determine the qualitative expression of quantitative insights. In other words, a data scientist is half business analyst, half data geek, and can use analysis to accurately answer key business and marketing questions. Data scientists understand that nowadays, data drives revenue. They're trained in subjects like statistics and advanced predictive analytics, and have experience working with big data sets.

DOs AND DON'Ts

Act soon. Paralysis and procrastination can be dangerous, especially if your market is competitive. Fill in your talent gaps. Tear down silos and start collaborating today.

Engage experienced third parties. Very few marketing organizations have the skills or talent on staff to meet the growing and evolving requirements of data-driven marketing. Consider augmenting your current team with expert third-party resources to teach your team new skills while executing and driving new approaches. This approach will deliver quick wins and move the organization and the business forward.

Establish a culture where employees are encouraged to fail fast—and safely. To be a change agent you will need to cultivate an environment of trust and an acceptance of failure. Learn as you go. Execute, evaluate, evolve.

Understand reality. Determine who in your organization excels at project management, data analysis, and team building. You won't be able to move forward until you optimize the talent around you.

Don't get paralyzed by hype or fear. Fretting over having to make a decision takes up too much valuable brain space, and you can't focus on the business if you're consumed with uncertainty. Don't put off changes, performance management, or organizational restructuring because they seem difficult. Naturally, you absolutely need to do your due diligence, but once the way forward is clear, take a breath, trust your gut, and act upon those difficult decisions.

Don't try old approaches in the new world of big data marketing. Build an organization that is customer-centric and well-staffed with technology and data experts. They're the ones who will help bring key customer acquisition and retention strategies to life through marketing.

The Five Steps to Data-Driven Marketing and Big Data Insights

6

Step One

Get Smart, Get Strategic

Source: © Teradata 2013

I met the chief marketing officer (CMO) of a well-known brand at the 2013 *Direct Marketing News* Marketing Hall of Femme in New York City. She told a story to a group of CMOs, chuckling as she recalled how the company CEO had burst into her office just a few weeks before. He began his fly-by by discussing how digital was changing the game for their industry, and then he quizzed her with a question from out-of-the-blue. "Have you heard about this thing called 'big data'?" he asked. The CMO said she laughed in response—of course she had. Next, he mandated that she and the organization needed to "do something!" about it. No worries. She was already on the case.

Yes, the headlines about big data continue to capture front page ink in the business section—and continue to spur a fever-pitch that can instill the dreaded deer-in-the-headlights response from even the most credible and stalwart members of the C-suite. But, does all the noise about big data sound a little familiar to you? To me, the stories have the ring of 1999 all over again. Who can forget the mad rush to dot.com—or should I say, *dot.gone*?

The current frenzy over big data reminds me of digital's early days because, once again, we're seeing the hype around the latest trend become so intense that it distracts business leaders and threatens to mask the actual value and opportunity the technological innovation can deliver. Of course, the fact that every vendor defines big data differently only adds to the confusion. My goal with this chapter is to clear up some of the uncertainty and help you establish a foundation, so you can dig in and identify the opportunities that big data and data-driven marketing can offer to you.

To recap what I've discussed in the previous chapters, here's what we know for certain:

- Over the next three to five years, digital disruption will profoundly transform businesses and consumer buying behaviors.
- Companies must adopt data-driven marketing to drive more relevant customer experiences and return more value to their corporations and organizations.
- Big data marketing will be a big disappointment if you don't implement it in focused, self-contained projects or as part of a larger strategic vision for the company.

So, the imperative for marketers is to adopt a data-driven marketing approach and leverage big data to drive relevant, real-time interactions.

Vision Leads to Strategy

Every solid strategy starts with a clear vision, but unfortunately, too many companies choose to skip over the *vision thing*. Then, since these companies lack vision, technology—not strategy—becomes the driver, and as I've seen time and time again, that's a recipe for disaster. Technology is never the panacea. It's the enabler. That's why aligning behind a shared vision is critical—and not only among the marketing department, but across the entire C-suite, as well. A shared vision paints the picture that the broader organization needs to support. It helps connect the dots on projects and helps illustrate how these projects drive value. And it can be the arbitrator to achieve alignment when change sparks turf wars.

Since every business is different, the starting points, the visions, and the final strategies will vary from marketing team to marketing team; however, there *are* common factors all organizations share. Once you've established the vision, it's time to work together with other senior leaders to develop a broad, comprehensive plan of attack. As you do, consider including these five fundamental components:

1. Customer interaction strategy
2. Analytics strategy
3. Data strategy
4. Organizational strategy
5. Technology strategy

Let me walk you through each one in more detail.

Customer Interaction Strategy

Your customer interaction strategy needs to transcend the enterprise and be constructed from the outside in before you translate it into an internal view. Why? Because no one wants to repeat the same mistakes that were made with customer relationship management (CRM). Remember how CRM was supposed to focus on the customer and building better relationships? Things didn't go as planned, did they? CRM became internally focused and ended up actually creating silos for customers. Besides that, today's customers don't want their relationships managed, anyway; they want to be in control.

Recently, I bought a pair of sunglasses online, but after they arrived and I tried them on, I realized they weren't for me. So, I decided to return them at the retailer in my local mall. What a headache! I was told I couldn't exchange the sunglasses because they were a different SKU number. This retailer's separate eCommerce and inventory systems created a silo that negatively impacted me, the customer. Is it any wonder *CustomerThink* found that more than 70 percent of CRM projects fail?[1] That's not only because the tactic itself falls short, but also because, as I mentioned, today's consumers don't want to be *managed*. Instead, they want control. They want a value-added experience, defined differently industry to industry and product to product. Big data marketing must be built on the foundation of this interaction mentality.

To develop a customer interaction strategy, you will need to map and understand the buyer journey, from first contact all the way through purchase and aftermarket relationships. You'll then have to map out the changes that need to occur across organizations, systems, and data to transform and deliver on your customer engagement plan.

Figure 6.1 shows what a continuous, customer-centric journey can look like in our data-driven world.

Years ago, I was involved with a company that prioritized customer experience as a cross-organizational focus. We established a cross-functional team, and this team was given the mandate to elevate the customer experience so the company could retain and grow its customer base. Once we identified what exactly the customer experience could mean, the team began two concurrent workstreams. The first was to map the current customer journey from first touch to aftermarket sales and service—and wow, was that an eye-opener. We identified more than 300 touchpoints across the customer experience journey! The first phase of the journey, acquisition, involved three interactions: online nurturing to drive automated digital conversations, teleprospecting calls, and service team communications via request for proposals (RFPs)—and that was only the beginning. Now I can assure you, 300 is an absurd number of touchpoints, and I have no doubt the brand's customers considered the buying journey painful, but after facing that reality and setting a vision for how the company wanted to innovate its customer experience, the cross-functional team was able to move forward and establish data, organizational, and technology strategies.

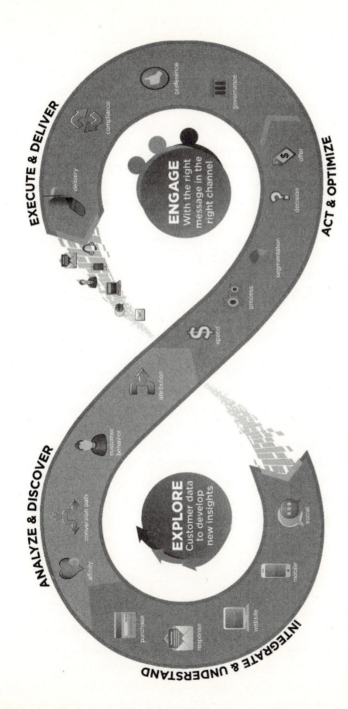

FIGURE 6.1 The Customer-Centric Journey

Source: © Teradata 2012

Analytics Strategy

Just like the word *data*, the term *analytics* continues to grow in importance as a competitive differentiator for businesses. Tom Davenport, who wrote the foreword to this book, is a leading global expert on business process reengineering and analytical competition, and he has defined three main categories of analytics.[2]

1. **Business analytics:** The conventional reports and intelligent dashboards that business leaders have advanced and embraced since the automation and capture of enterprise information and key performance indicators (KPIs).
2. **Predictive analytics:** The use of data from past and present, and the application of statistical models to predict what may happen based on past events.
3. **Prescriptive analytics:** The insights that tell you what to do. Examples of prescriptive analytics include optimization, simulations on pricing, and interaction approaches.

Because data and technology will fuel analytics, it is important to identify where you are currently and what type of analytics you need to compete and better position your organization in this age of digital disruption. Chapter 9 provides an overview into metrics and what is essential to consider in the era of data-driven marketing. I'd also recommend books like *Keeping Up with the Quants: Your Guide to Understanding and Using Analytics*, by Tom Davenport and Jinho Kim; *Competing on Analytics: The New Science of Winning*, by Tom Davenport and Jeanne Harris; and *Taming the Big Data Tidal Wave*, by Bill Franks.

Data Strategy

Given the traditional silos of information across the enterprise, and the fact that data-driven marketing requires credible data, the development of an enterprise-wide data strategy is absolutely critical. I'll discuss this in more detail in Chapter 8, "Untangle the Data Hairball," but it is important to note that in order for your data strategy to be actionable, it needs to permeate the enterprise, and it needs to be driven as a partnership between IT, marketing, and other key business functions. In addition, you'll need to link the data strategy to overall business objectives, garner senior level sponsorship, stay mindful of data management issues such as data hygiene and compliance considerations, and be certain you have the organizational talent to execute. That sounds like an impossible-to-achieve laundry list. But leading marketing organization *are* making it happen. They're breaking down the changes into manageable pieces and making progress step-by-step.

For example, as I discussed in Chapter 3, while the American Red Cross moved from vision to strategy, Peggy Dyer, the American Red Cross's visionary CMO, realized the company lacked the internal expertise to drive a holistic data strategy. She gained broad internal support and senior management's commitment to data as a key strategic asset before she hired a vice president of data strategy. Then, she and her marketing team waited to finalize their strategy until after that leader joined the organization. Dyer knew the American Red Cross's data problem was bigger than her team could solve, and she knew they needed a *been-there, done-that* leader.

Another best practice I've seen for tackling data strategy is to ensure all customer and prospective buyer data, especially big data, is not locked in a silo. To put it another way, all of your company's data must be part of this overarching, enterprise-wide data strategy. A chief information officer (CIO) from a large financial services organization said it best when she and I met to discuss her organization's data challenges. She was new in her role, and she shared her concerns about the fragmentation of the company's customer data—in fact, she described it as "data everywhere." She told me that the company needed to bring all these silos together and that big data had to be a part of it. Then, there needed to be an integrated strategy to map the data back to overall business objectives.

Integrated Strategy

This savvy CIO was right, of course. Tackling big data must be a part of the broader data strategy. Remember, we don't want to make the same mistakes we did when eCommerce became a disruptor and created silos of customer experience and more fragmented consumer and buyer data. Because big data inputs and outcomes are important, the processes and workstreams involving them must be part of a broader, enterprise-wide data strategy, and you *must* integrate them accordingly. If you don't tackle the job holistically, then you'll simply reconstruct the painful silos and further fragment the customer experience.

I spoke with Jim Sturm, President and CEO of Brierley+Partners, a strategic marketing technology services provider, about what he sees in working with consumer-facing brands to help them engage more effectively using data. Sturm says, "Brands want to know how to harness the power of data held in disparate locations throughout their organizations to deliver on consumer expectations and bring insights from that data as close to the customer. Non-transactional behavior should be identifiable and tied to a customer, and unstructured data must be mined for deeper, actionable insights."[3]

Let's drill a little deeper into big data strategy as part of a broader strategy. Every CMO I meet with wants to discuss big data, and the one question I am asked the most is: Where do most people start?

Most organizations start with a business objective that's focused on the customer journey. Some are working to understand the key points in the *path to purchase* or *golden path* terms to describe the sequence of offline and online interactions that occurred to affect a transaction such as a sale. Others are focused on understanding customer attrition or churn, the path of interactions that led to a defecting customer. Regardless of whether you choose to focus on new customer acquisition or customer attrition, another key best practice is to begin with a pilot and, as I explain below, you need to make that pilot well-defined, with a short time frame and clear, tangible outcomes.

Defined and Finite Pilots

A big data project is no different from any other IT project, and, as I'm sure you've heard before, if the technology is new, it's always best to start small. A small pilot project allows you to get your feet wet using the technology so you can then determine what you will need in terms of support from IT. It also allows end users to see the analytical capabilities that big data presents, and it gives IT and end users the opportunity to optimize collaboration for great analytics results.

A large financial services company I know used a big data pilot project to better understand why levels of customer churn were so high. The team, led by an expert in customer insights within the company, used the pilot to holistically analyze all on- and offline channels, including the call center, physical locations, and digital platforms. The pilot had a well-defined outcome—to identify the key triggers in customer churn—and it was also time-constrained to end in 60 days. Ultimately, this financial services brand identified two triggers that led to customer churn and then took action on those results to affect future customer interaction strategies.

Organizational Strategy

Since big data transcends departmental walls and challenges conventional approaches, it is disrupting traditional organizational structures and silos. As a result, the C-suite needs to work together to revisit organizational models, evaluate current structures, and design new approaches to maximize revenue growth in this new world. As I write this book, most companies are only beginning to understand the organizational design opportunities presented by big data marketing, and I predict we will see this area advance rapidly to become a critical change management imperative for CEOs and presidents. That said, I *am* seeing trends for you to consider as you work to innovate how you go to market and dismantle the internal empires that undermine the customer experience.

Different Teams, Same Goal

Collaboration is key. As Ginger Conlon, editor-in-chief at *Direct Marketing News*, explains, "Many business leaders are consumed by capturing actionable data from outside their organization—as they should be. But not to the point of overlooking the reams of invaluable data they already own." And what's the best way to access that internal data, and then integrate it with external data? You need to work together across departments, Conlon says. To foster this kind of collaboration, she recommends a few specific approaches, such as creating shared goals, aligning existing goals and compensation, and launching a pilot to demonstrate the benefits and results each team—and the organization as a whole—can gain from sharing their data and collaborating. Keep at it, and your efforts to establish a more collaborative enterprise are likely to pay off in a big way. According to PricewaterhouseCoopers's (PwC's) "5th Annual Global Digital IQ Survey," strong collaborators are four times as likely as other teams to lead in innovation and margin and revenue growth.[4]

In Chapter 7, "Tear Down the Silos," I'll discuss collaboration at length, but let me stress this now: Cross-pollination, or equipping marketing with dedicated implants from other organizations like customer insights or IT, can assist in executing cross-functional initiatives. In fact, I find that more and more companies are driving this organizational matrix approach with hardline and dotted-line reporting structures, unifying formerly disparate teams. As I discussed in Chapter 5, in some companies, IT resources and customer insights are now distributed within marketing and other business functions, and they report back to a cross-enterprise team that sits in operations or finance. Down the road, we may even see these teams report to a new chief customer experience officer. And why not? The analysis contributed by a customer insights team is more important than ever before. These professionals, known for their quant skills and ability to build predictive models, will be critical in understanding, applying, and leveraging big data insights to drive more valuable customer interactions.

In the future, we'll also see more emphasis on collaboration between the CMO and the CIO, a trend that has been steadily building over the past few years. Marketing, as always, is charged with driving innovative customer engagement. But nowadays, technology is at the center of virtually all marketing processes and strategies. So, as I explained earlier in Chapter 5, it makes perfect sense for the CIO and the CMO to become strategic partners, working together to drive business value.

Skills Assessment

Big data marketing and a data-driven approach require new types of expertise across your organization, and that alone can be incentive for restructuring. I recommend evaluating data, analytical, and collaboration skills broadly across your key customer-facing organizations so you can identify and understand any gaps. Then, fill in those gaps with consultants, strategic partners, and strong hiring so you take steps forward.

Technology Strategy

Successful organizations not only nurture strategic partnerships between the CMO and CIO, but also marry business and technology strategy. Then, when debates or roadblocks emerge in these companies, the CIO and CMO can use the broader vision to continue to drive change. Unfortunately, I've seen far too many times that a business strategy developed in isolation from the supporting technology can get derailed with even slight provocation. So, even though I realize every organization has its own framework for technology strategy, I suggest you consider the following three elements in your discussion and strategy setting:

1. Outsourced versus in-house customer engagement strategy
2. Consolidation or point solutions
3. Short-term and mid-term roadmaps

Outsourced versus In-House Customer Engagement Strategy

Your technology strategy will vary depending upon where the data is and who is driving the marketing interaction experience. In the past, many firms relied on marketing service providers to manage their data and to create and execute the campaigns that drive the interactions. Why? Perhaps the hairball was too convoluted within the company, or the expertise was not present, or both. Of course, outsourcing like this can be a strong strategy to augment talent gaps and to speed time to market; however, many companies are now choosing to bring these key functions in-house, even if they continue to work with a third-party expert to help. What's driving firms to pull this back? I see four main reasons:

1. The high cost of data and marketing execution services
2. Gaps in data that outside service providers can't close, and that the company itself is best poised to augment and manage
3. The latency or lag time to execute time-sensitive campaigns or capitalize on real-time insights for better interactions
4. Better understanding by companies that data management is a strategic asset to own

Consolidated Platforms or Siloed Point Solutions

I've been in high-tech applications for 25 years, and I know the ultimate inflection point when I see it. The ultimate inflection point happens when applications have matured, and IT and business leaders need to decide whether they consolidate and integrate applications, or continue to integrate and leverage multiple point solutions. We are at that point with marketing technology.

As I'm sure you know, point solutions are everywhere: email systems that require manual list loads from campaign management systems; project management systems that track line items but not the creative review process; standalone spreadsheets to manage spend that remain disconnected from financial systems and require weeks for finance and marketing operations teams to sort out whenever it's time for the budget alignment exercise. Unlike sales departments, which use integrated suites like salesforce.com or Siebel to manage the business of sales, marketing and IT need to evaluate the benefit of an integrated marketing platform to manage the core fundamentals, such as budgets, workflows, campaigns, and segmentation.

Short-term and Mid-term Roadmaps

Many CMOs I know have hired their own vice president of customer experience or customer engagement. This person is typically excellent at identifying the business requirements to innovate the customer experience and can work internally to evolve the technology and organizational training needed to transform that experience. Once again, the American Red Cross serves as a great model for this new role. The American Red Cross's Vice President of CRM, Banefsheh Ghassemi, worked with the CMO to construct short- and mid-term technology roadmaps that mapped back to the organization's vision and overall strategies. While a long-term roadmap still has its purpose, today's C-suite needs to deliver quick wins. Short- and mid-term roadmaps help turn vision into action. They also help keep teams motivated with the celebration of milestones reached and visible progress.

As the stories from the American Red Cross and the financial services company demonstrate, savvy business executives and their marketing teams aren't falling victim to the big data hype. You won't catch them with the deer-in-the-headlights stare. Instead, they're tackling the challenges that big data marketing poses by joining forces with IT and data experts to set a vision, build a comprehensive, multifaceted strategy, and execute one step at a time.

DOs AND DON'Ts

Get started. There's no need for panic, but there's no reason to delay, either. What *one thing* can you do today to move your company out of the Dark Ages and into the Enlightened Age of Data? For instance, would identifying the path to purchase help you improve your marketing effectiveness? Would hiring a data strategist provide you with expertise and process to drive the change? Too many times, marketers try to boil the ocean when all we need to do is get one drink of success to validate and fuel change.

Keep learning. Start with a vision and a business case, but always keep this top-of-mind: The journey to a data-driven marketing model will illuminate new questions and fresh ways of looking at strategies. As you uncover new data and trends, remind yourself that you don't know what you don't know, and be open to the discoveries and opportunities you encounter along the way.

Develop strategies for customer interaction, data, organizational, and technology approaches. You can't boil the ocean, but a holistic vision and strategy across all lines of business will better position you for success. Ensure these strategies have senior executive ownership and alignment, and that there is a broader business objective to tie it all together. If you establish that foundation, there will be a unified mission pulling everyone forward when change becomes difficult.

Don't expect a quick fix. Using big data marketing is not like waiting for Zoltar, the retro mechanical genie featured in the movie *Big*, to spit out a card with the answers. You can't plug in some data and then come to work the next day to find that your wish has been granted. Big data insights may take time to emerge, and the process is continually evolving.

Don't rely on traditional approaches. The world of data-driven marketing and big data marketing is new and different. Consumers and buyers are different, too. Now is the time to

(*continued*)

(*continued*)

step back, look at the big picture and ask tough questions, and experiment with different approaches. I often find that, as business leaders, we don't experiment enough. Big data pilots are all about experimenting and learning, and I encourage you to do the same with other projects, as well.

7

Step Two

Tear Down the Silos

1. Get Smart
   Get Strategic

2. Tear Down
   the Silos

3. Untangle
   the Data Hairball

4. Make Metrics
   Your Mantra

5. Process
   Is the New Black

5 Marketing **Steps**

Source: © Teradata 2013

've met with thousands of marketers during my decade as a chief marketing officer (CMO). I've listened to marketing leaders share war stories over dinners, during panel discussions, at keynotes, or in private chats. I've heard how they are working to transform their organizations to provide better customer experiences and fuel revenue growth in the Enlightened Age of Data. Their efforts go far beyond traditional repositioning; these change agents are actually recreating their organizations. They know tearing down proverbial corporate silos is critical to enable the interdepartmental collaboration and alignment required to gain the full value from data-driven marketing.

While they are reinventing the marketing function to be data-driven, these C-level executives face some mighty obstacles across the organization. Roadblocks, bottlenecks, and detours can slow or even derail a change initiative, and in order to keep moving forward, it's not uncommon for CMOs and their teams to find themselves challenging the status quo, bucking convention, and testing cultural boundaries. Once complete, the transformations are often considered confidential and the strategies proprietary. Why? Because the evolution proves integral to driving value and gaining a competitive advantage. I tip my hat to these change agents; tearing down corporate silos can be professionally risky and personally draining.

The need for change agents to tear down silos has never been greater. Boards of directors and CEOs crave business leaders who can navigate change and demonstrate results, and the hunger for information about how to drive collaboration and innovation has sparked a flurry of white papers, articles, and books. Ranjay Gulati, PhD, a Harvard professor and leading academic in the field of organizational behavior, addresses this issue in his well-known article, "The Four Cs of Customer-Focused Solutions." Gulati cites lack of communication, narrow focus and view, and conventional organizational models as primary obstacles for business leaders to build a more customer-centric and responsive organization.

Gulati strongly advises C-level executives to be change agents. He says they need to foster an environment of collaboration, coordination, and connection, as well as demonstrate the capability to be a generalist (someone who is able to work effectively across internal departmental boundaries) as opposed to a specialist.

According to Gulati, the ultimate goal is to provide compelling customer experiences. In reality, modern enterprises have been built from the inside out versus outside-in. As Gulati explains, "In most companies, knowledge and expertise reside in distinct units—organized by product, service, or geography. To deliver customer-focused solutions, companies need mechanisms that allow customer-related information sharing, division of labor, and decision making to occur easily across company boundaries." It is imperative for CMOs to activate their teams behind a more compelling customer engagement strategy and drive cross-functional initiatives that require them to break down silos across the broader organization.[1]

But before marketers attempt changes to the enterprise, they need to tackle changes within their own marketing organization.

Tearing Down Silos Internal to Marketing

Take a look around your marketing department. Odds are, it's stretched taffy thin and people are running so fast that they are hyper-focused on their own domain and projects. Now, look again—this time, more closely. Do these dynamics create division? Do these divisions help or hurt the productivity and effectiveness of your marketing efforts? In many cases, internal silos create needless complexity and perpetuate problems.

Unifying marketing within the company is crucial, and your efforts should focus on collaboration, consolidation, and organization.

Collaboration

Collaboration and getting team members to see the big picture is critical to the modern marketing department's success. "Collaboration across teams and departments is essential to getting the unique insight that can provide a competitive edge," says Ginger Conlon, editor-in-chief of *Direct Marketing News*. She points out that, according to PricewaterhouseCoopers's "5th Annual Global Digital IQ Survey," 83 percent of strong collaborators say that harnessing big data will give their organization a competitive advantage, versus only 65 percent of other respondents.[2]

Conlon notes that individual teams such as marketing, customer service, and sales often have unique customer data sets that, if combined, could help improve overall performance and build customer engagement with more relevant, timely interactions and communications. As an example, she cites a law firm whose marketing team and partners share client data to determine which clients are the best referrers. The marketers use that insight to cultivate those relationships and, as a result, they have seen significant increases in referrals and new clients from those referrals. Another example is Citibank, which uses data from its Thank You rewards program to support cross-selling in the contact center. ("I see you have

X thank-you points. If you apply for *Y* product with me now, we'll add another *X* points, which will bring you to *Z* level.")

Where should you start? As your first step, I'd suggest determining your goal and discerning who on your team can best achieve it. Not every employee is wired to collaborate, and early misfires can derail both the process and the synergy. Once you are confident you have the right leadership identified, you will need alignment from your peers on the guiding principles that will set the stage for positive collaboration. From there, look broadly across the organization to include delegates from key stakeholder organizations who can best support the goal or enhance its chance for success. To successfully drive value, collaboration requires purposeful focus from senior leaders all the way to cross-functional teams.

Consolidation

Consolidation can be divided into four main areas: 1) alignment of vision/ objectives, 2) integration and consolidation of data, 3) unification of internal marketing department activities, and 4) consolidation of systems and processes.

1. **Alignment of vision/objectives:** The most important part of consolidation is deciding what is not integral to your company's long-term vision. In other words, you'll need to map your customer interaction and data strategies to shared objectives and milestones, and then track, report, and test along the way to show value and progress. When I was a marketing executive at Oracle, I learned the expression "high escalation and low frustration." You, too, may find it helpful to keep teams focused and moving forward.

2. **Integration and consolidation of data:** Even marketing departments have data silos. For instance, many marketing departments have a separate team responsible for their digital or social media initiatives. While that team may be tracking digital interactions or the sentiment of a customer's social media interactions with the brand, the true value from that data isn't realized until it is integrated with data from other channels, like offline purchase history or call center transactions. Of course, the customer engagement side of marketing tells only part of the story. You also need consolidation and integration of data between teams from marketing, finance, and so on.

3. **Unification of internal marketing department activities:** Uniting behind shared objectives across the department and aligning teams to

produce collective results helps connect marketing teams and eliminate artificial barriers. Because large global marketing departments produce thousands of projects every fiscal year, it can be extremely difficult for marketers to keep current will all that is going on across their departments. In fact, nearly 65 percent of marketers in the *Global Teradata Data-Driven Marketing Survey, 2013* reported silos within the marketing department prevent them from having a holistic view of campaigns and other marketing activities. A unified marketing platform helps eliminate confusion and improves visibility.

4. **Consolidation of systems and processes**: Systems and processes are notorious silo enhancers because they help create empires, fragment data, and slow down innovation. Consolidation of internal systems and processes with purpose-built systems unifies data, people, and technology, and reduces costs, as well.

Organization

Organization—or should I say reorganization?—is essential to moving forward to the Enlightened Age of Data; however, many find it difficult and uncomfortable to rethink the bastions of marketing. Companies have built and maintained internal silos—like those that exist between corporate communications and the digital team, or the database marketer and the email marketer—over the course of years, even decades. Indeed, marketing specialists earned their credentials by isolating themselves so they could drive value through results in their interaction channel of focus. But don't forget, years ago, marketers were able to manually integrate data, channels, and lead management. Back in the '80s and '90s, there were only a few interaction channels, and content and campaigns could thrive even *if* they were fragmented throughout different parts of the organization.

Clearly, times have changed, and modern marketing demands a different approach. Just be careful: Sometimes a "different approach" can lead to increased fragmentation. CMOs need to stay vigilant while they're reorganizing, so that the varied skill sets and personalities of today's new talent—the digital guru, the up-and-coming social media maven, the analytical product marketer, and the rising PR star—don't end up creating new silos and complicating internal dynamics even more. It can be difficult to align today's teams on strategic initiatives and messages, and to manage intricate executions, when multiple hand-off points have the potential to negatively impact quality and timing.

Some forward-thinking companies are hurdling challenges like these, and in many firms, exciting transformations are already underway. One great example is that the function of marketing communications departments is evolving into a new way to communicate within the company. In the past, an independent marketing communications team created artificial barriers, sluggish turnaround times, and multiple layers of control. Now, savvy CMOs are moving to replace or augment this function with the broader role of *content marketing* that spans across *all* internal marketing departments. Content marketing's job is to develop and release aligned messages for customers.

For example, the CMO of inContact, Mariann McDonagh, replaced her entire corporate communications team with a new content marketing group staffed by veteran journalists and media mavens who are used to ferreting out a great story and reporting it with a fresh perspective. Her purpose was not to perpetuate conventional corporate communications deliverables like brochures and whitepapers that often sit on a virtual shelf and collect virtual dust. Instead, her focus was to help the brand become a true publisher of compelling, valued-added materials that are customized to the audience or buyer persona and driven across a variety of content channels. That goal requires a shift away from agency-like messaging and other content that has not translated well in our digital age, and it depends on experienced professionals who can create relevant, crisp content for publication across multiple channels. These storytellers cut across marketing department lines and use rich and multichannel media to parse company content for market consumption.

Tearing Down Silos between Marketing and Other Lines of Business

Once you've peered into your marketing department, widen your lens and look at the structure of your company as a whole. Once again, you'll probably find plenty of monolithic, function-based groups, each working in relative isolation, faithfully protecting its turf and staunchly defending its resources.

Collaboration

Collaboration is critical across all levels. In addition to having the CEO, COO, or president on board to help drive cross-enterprise change, the CMO also has to focus on building partnerships that will bring down the walls. Silos that separate marketing from IT, sales, and/or legal can be especially damaging, particularly for financial services, pharmaceutical companies, and others with strict compliance requirements.

For instance, let's focus on the gap between marketing and legal for a minute. How often does your marketing department use a simple email to throw materials over the wall for legal approval? Not only is this method inefficient; it also fails to provide an audit trail and could leave your company at risk of noncompliance. Savvy companies are improving collaboration with legal to provide better visibility to marketing projects, and they're using software tools to automate, collect, and record reviews and approvals. And of course, beyond legal, there will always be trouble when marketing, sales, customer insights, and finance don't communicate.

I recently had lunch with David Bonalle, the Director of Marketing and Customer insights for KeyBank, one of the nation's largest banks. As we talked, Bonalle shared with me the innovative moves KeyBank took to ensure silos came down. The first step—and a big reason why Bonalle joined KeyBank from American Express—was the decision made by the president of KeyBank, Bill Koehler, to transform the entire organization into an insights-driven enterprise. That decision laid the groundwork to improve collaboration and consolidate analytics functions across the organization. The second step was to ensure KeyBank embraced a data-driven marketing approach by consolidating marketing and customer insights under Bonalle's leadership. This bold organizational move put Bonalle, a long-time data-driven marketing executive, at the helm of a unified marketing and insights team reporting directly to the president. The consolidation was purposeful and signified that data-driven customer insights would drive the business forward, and that marketing would be driven by data, too.[3]

We've made collaboration a priority at Teradata Applications, as well. Here, we established a cross-functional team, the Demand Gen Council, to align sales and marketing, and this one move has had a huge impact on our department. The internal council was formed to enable the various teams within marketing to efficiently stay informed on all the department's initiatives, and a biweekly conference call gathers team members from our demand generation, applications strategy, sales, marketing operations, marketing finance, field deployment, data, and media teams. During each meeting we work to align our messaging strategy with our demand-generation execution and pitch, we prioritize overall campaign ideas, and we fine-tune the timing and logistics of executing initiatives. The sales department joins regularly to provide the input needed to prioritize programs and to drive alignment based on what they see in the market. While it may seem like this conference call could become unproductive, a strong leader, a tight agenda, and the clarity of each individual's role tears down the silos. Teradata Applications' Demand Gen Council has been enormously helpful; it ensures we are effectively leveraging our campaigns to drive revenue and retention programs, and it helps keep every initiative aligned with our overall messaging and strategy.

Ask marketers who have eliminated cross-functional barriers, and they'll tell you that one of the most important factors for success is robust communication. I'd wager they'd also advise you to identify ways to use automation like marketing workflows and financial tracking tools to keep communication focused and flowing between departments. It is now rare for any marketing process to stay within one team or function, so why not use workflow and financial tools, as well as purposeful communications, to facilitate collaboration?

Consolidation

Consolidation of data, processes, and workflow will help your organization move out of the Dark Ages. More specifically, you must identify where customer data lies across the business and integrate that data to create a single view of all interactions your customers have with your company. Most marketers believe that improved interdepartmental consolidation should be one of their top priorities; however, many are still struggling to develop that kind of understanding and insight. In fact, 82 percent of marketers in the *Global Teradata Data-Driven Marketing Survey, 2013* reported they do not routinely have a single view of all customer actions. For example, while demographic data may be gathered and kept by marketing, support call notes are likely documented by the customer service representatives, and inventory stock-out statistics are recorded by operations.

Organization

Organization helps facilitate collaboration—but some companies are going well beyond that. They're looking at radical, enterprise-wide changes to drive more cross-marketing synergies. For instance, even though the organizational location of customer insights can vary in large business-to-consumer (B2C) companies—I've seen it within marketing, R&D, IT, operations, and even finance—its role is generally that of an informant, not the one who ultimately calls the shots. However, as marketing becomes more data-driven, there may be a shift to customer insights actually leading marketing.

While this may sound "out there," at first, let's go back to the KeyBank example. Not only did KeyBank need to integrate marketing and data, but the company also had to help marketing and customer insights champion change across the broader organization. Koehler knew the transformation of marketing would be challenging, so early on, he expressed his personal support for both Bonalle and the company's commitment to become an insights-driven organization. As you might expect, having the president's focus and support helped knock down obstacles and fast-track decisions when needed. For instance, Koehler's senior-level sponsorship was invaluable when analytics showed that a major acquisition marketing campaign was not effective. Even though some people wanted to stay the course despite the analytics, Koehler reiterated his commitment to remaining insights-driven, and the marketing campaign was completely revamped to reflect the new findings.

Developing a Strategic Framework for Synergy

How can you improve interaction and collaboration across disparate groups? What exact steps can you take, starting today? First, you need to develop a strategic framework that will drive synergy with other departments and help you align for both short-term and long-term success. To help you begin the process, I've identified four ways you can prime both the communication and execution channels:

1. **Determine the vision and goal.** Develop and communicate a shared understanding of expectations, goals, and anticipated returns. Align on definitions, as well as roles and responsibilities.
2. **Make everyone a part of marketing.** Collaborate. Empower team members from other organizations to become active participants in setting performance goals and contributing to your go-to-market campaign development process. Then create communication channels for rich, two-way exchanges of information and ideas, so every customer-facing function can deliver your message to customers and prospects—and then return data to you for further nurturing. Some

companies use circulated reports with scheduled cross-functional team meetings. Others will make this a standing topic in quarterly or operational meetings. A third option is to create an internal collaboration platform like Jive or Chatter to provide real-time updates to the appropriate team(s).

3. **Remain transparent.** Be sure the vision you developed above permeates the entire marketing effort. Keep the other departments up-to-date by making revisions to the marketing calendar, and add those revisions to the seed list for your campaigns. Transparency between sales and marketing is especially essential. It enables sales to provide you with the feedback you need to fine-tune and optimize marketing initiatives.

4. **Share what you did.** Communicate results with the entire company to generate a macro-view of accomplishments. Let everyone know where opportunities exist and which improvements have been made. Once you show finance how you can drive improvement in marketing returns or demonstrate to sales how your leads are moving through the pipeline, you can start working together to increase revenue and reduce the overall cost per lead.

New Best Friends: The CMO and the CIO

I have to end this chapter with a discussion of the biggest, most important silo-busting imperative of them all: Marketing must join forces with IT.

As long as I've been a marketer, I've witnessed the fly-bys and finger-pointing that occur between my department and IT. Marketers hide servers under their desks, and then groan when they need IT to fix various problems. IT can't figure out why marketing always waits until the last minute and yet wants everything *tomorrow*.

Sometimes, the stereotypes even permeate the C-suite. I've heard CMOs described as the right-brain of the enterprise, and chief information officers (CIOs) as the left. I've also heard CMOs don't know when to say "no," and CIOs never say "yes." Others complain that CMOs sprint ahead too fast, while CIOs plod along too slow. The list of grievances goes on and on, but like all stereotypes, these are based on generalized misconceptions, and when they're continually reinforced, they do nothing more than divide marketing and IT into two camps: us versus them. This simple-minded approach is terribly counterproductive for CMOs today.

Granted, marketing and IT *are* different disciplines—and CMOs and CIOs have traditionally approached problems in different ways. However, marketers absolutely *need* modern technology to improve processes and deliver data-driven, integrated campaigns with higher ROMI. Smart CMOs will realize the importance of quickly healing any rift that exists between marketing and IT.

Why? Because the customer experience is now the force behind most marketing and business strategies, and technology is core to the customer experience—today more than ever before. Therefore, marketing and IT are inextricably linked. There's really no other logical conclusion, and the imperative for CMO-CIO alignment has never been higher.

As I first mentioned in Chapter 4, Gartner is predicting that CMOs will be outspending their counterpart CIOs on technology by 2017, and that forecast simply reinforces my point. A robust, strategic relationship between the CMO and CIO is essential to ensure that marketers leverage IT's resources and expertise to advance the customer experience. I can't imagine staying relevant without it.

Let me stress this again, too: The entire enterprise needs to align on common terms and goals. For instance, if everyone is aware of the company's IT portfolio, then employees can create incredibly useful integrations of data, and those are much more valuable than the perspective gleaned from the single application marketing purchased on its own firsthand. Even so, it will take more than lip service or one project to build these kinds of relationships. Marketers must be willing to engage early with the CIO and build a trusted relationship based on data and the end goal of the customer experience. For their part, IT professionals must be willing to understand the dynamic of marketing and help align to its fast pace.

At Teradata, we are undergoing a marketing transformation, and now IT and marketing increasingly rely on one another to help adopt a global, data-driven marketing approach. Before, the two groups approached projects in two different ways. But we're all becoming increasingly aware that we need to be on *the same team* to help accelerate the application of technology. Our CEO combined the marketing and IT organizations together and tapped a seasoned executive to manage them both. Our shared goal? To improve our marketing through the expression of our technology, both internally and in the marketplace.

Companies are also hiring data scientists to help bridge the gap between marketing and IT. As I mentioned in Chapter 5, data scientists are a new breed of business leaders. They're trained in subjects like statistics and advanced predictive analytics, and they understand that today, *data drives revenue*. Data scientists recognize that marketing operations are strategic, and they work to craft the qualitative expression of quantitative insights for widespread use across the company.

Everyone throughout the enterprise can benefit from the efforts of data scientists and all those in marketing and IT. After all, marketing is no longer a department within the business; marketing *is* the business. In today's dynamic environment of rapidly proliferating channels and variable internal constraints, many companies are struggling to track, better understand, and respond to what consumers want, need, and expect. Integration and collaboration among all core business functions are essential to meeting those goals.

DOs AND DON'Ts

CMOs: Take your counterpart CIO out to lunch. Make the call. Think about what shared objectives you have and how you can work together better. Use the interaction over lunch to start building a stronger relationship. I guarantee you'll be pleasantly surprised by all you have in common.

Find common ground. Remember, everyone in the C-suite can talk the same language: the language of driving business growth.

Don't expect changes overnight. The walls separating departments are high and wide in many companies. Plan for an ongoing conversation. Think of transformation and innovation as marathons—not sprints.

Don't rely on traditional roles and responsibilities. Hire marketing staff with IT expertise, and hire IT staff with marketing expertise. Create teams that can *communicate* with each other. Provide education and training for your existing team members to help them expand their perspective and understanding of both marketing and technology.

8

Step Three

Untangle the Data Hairball

Source: © Teradata 2013

I'll be the first to admit it. Hairballs are disgusting. As any pet owner will tell you, they cause indigestion, gagging . . . and worse. So, why would I choose the word *hairball* to describe marketing's big data problem? I use it precisely because it elicits such a visceral response and because whenever I first mention the data hairball to a roomful of marketers, I sense immediate recognition. Heads start nodding in agreement. Nervous smiles appear. Some people shuffle their feet as if they could sidestep the very thought of it. Audiences know exactly what I'm talking about when I use the term, and that doesn't surprise me at all.

Marketers are on the front lines, battling the chaos of traditional and digital information that accumulates 24/7. They're the ones who recognize the enormous complexity of the situation. They're the ones who feel the knot of anxiety in their stomachs when they're called into the C-suite to present strategies that often lack the supporting data needed to make a compelling case.

Former Kodak Chief Marketing Officer (CMO) Jeffrey Hayzlett, who now serves as an advisor to other CMOs and CEOs, admitted to me when we were discussing data-driven marketing in the spring of 2013 that he knew the hairball all too well, and that he had struggled with it at Kodak.

"I was coughing up the data hairball every day," Hayzlett said during our conversation. "At the time, Kodak had unique lines of business focused on their markets, printers, cameras—just to name a couple. Each of those divisions had siloed information they simply weren't sharing effectively across the enterprise. All I wanted to do was answer the following simple question, 'What are the names of the 1,500 customers who purchased one of our high-value printers?'"[1]

That's the data hairball.

Hayzlett laughed. "If someone asked me to produce that list with 24 hour notice or else they'd kill my children, I'd be childless today. I couldn't have come up with those names. The systems were broken, even though the data did exist," he said. "Oh yeah, I coughed up the data hairball. We all did."

Hayzlett was facing a very common problem. He couldn't see all the interactions of one customer across all the channels.

"Everything was so siloed. I had one division selling someone a camera, another division selling someone a printer, another division selling someone a keepsake photo book . . . yet it was the same customer, and they looked at the company as one entity," he recalled. "But, I have three different warranties, three different ways Kodak was marketing to them, and I had no way to look across those siloes at that particular person."

Early on, Hayzlett hired a chief data officer to put in a framework and tie all the systems together. And, of course, his story at Kodak isn't an isolated case.

Modern marketing is consumed with the data hairball right now, and CMOs and their teams are lying awake at night, wondering how they're going to untangle the mess. They want to know how to make sense of all. They want to access the data and use it to be more effective and efficient. They need to know how to apply big data analytics to inform their marketing messages; to test new, real-time interaction strategies; and to innovate their marketing engagement. And of course, they want to know how they can stop the data hairball from growing more tangled given the constant influx and growth of information.

Start with Talent

For years, I've been advising business leaders about their efforts to improve engagement and relevant digital interactions with their targeted audience. I can't tell you the number of times CMOs have confided that they needed to stop projects to hire the necessary talent. Too many of us think we can get by with the team we have, only to discover that we need more specialized skills to untangle the data hairball and drive a successful outcome. Hayzlett realized he needed to hire a chief data officer, but other CMOs have solved the problem in different, and yet similar, ways. For example, Peggy Dyer, the CMO of the American Red Cross, also understands the critical importance of talent. Dyer actually put her donor engagement initiatives on hold until she hired a vice president of data strategy to help guide the process.[2]

Hayzlett and Dyer chose to hire external candidates; however, sometimes the talent may be sitting within the broader company. KeyBank, one of the nation's largest bank-based financial services companies, needed to bring more insight to their marketing functions. The company's president found the talent internally; he appointed the head of customer insights to run marketing and connect the bank's data collection and customer engagement efforts.

One last note about talent: Do not, under any circumstances, outsource your data strategy. Outsourcing certain data-analysis *execution* tasks is common and acceptable, but the *strategy* must be owned internally. Remember: Data is now a competitive differentiator. Data and actionable insights are quickly becoming the core of every company's competitive advantage. Therefore, you need someone on your team, at a senior level, to help drive the data strategy and ensure employees across your organization are dedicated to executing it.

Silos Can Threaten Big Data Strategy

C-level support is also essential to the success of any big data strategy. Why? Because many brands are still working to develop a consolidated view of their customers, and, all too often, that work becomes a struggle. Then, without strong executive leadership, this struggle can pit departments against one another, and give rise to internal turf wars. Maybe that's not surprising, considering that customer data is typically collected and owned by a variety of different departments. Marketing collects demographic data; product/customer support keeps customer satisfaction data; finance captures transactional purchase data; and so on. Plus, IT is usually involved in data management and control across multiple departments, which means that IT often also has ultimate ownership over data. In fact, Teradata's recent research shows that less than one-third of marketers own and control customer data, while more than half rely on IT to access their data. In addition to validating the need for partnership between the CMO and the chief information officer (CIO), these results indicate how crippled data-driven marketing would be in a company that can't squash turf wars and smash through interdepartmental silos.

I'm a realist, and I understand that turf wars will always exist to some extent. As Hayzlett says, "Wherever you have people and systems, there *will* be turf wars." For me, the key is to rise above them. Here's a tip from Hayzlett's playbook: "Be clear what business objectives you are trying to drive," he advises. "Emphasize that you're there to serve the company, to help the company deliver on the promises you all agreed to make. That is what the focus should be on—what the group is trying to accomplish—not what's yours or what's theirs. This approach disarms the turf war, since turf wars break out around personal issues."

Using this technique to achieve alignment across his organization, Hayzlett met with his peers and made it clear their focus should be on how fixing the data problem would drive business results. Then, whenever an internal dynamic threatened to derail his team and the mission, he would revisit the project goals, lay out the obstacles, and remind the other C-suiters of the overarching business objective. His role as a change agent was about getting people on the same page and keeping them there, focused on the bigger picture.

Over the years, I've learned that internal dynamics can create the most stubborn obstacles marketers face. They can slow down, impede, and potentially kill any attempts at change. Many large brands have been striving to fix their tangled data for years, and yet they continue to fail, often because they cannot overcome internal obstacles. The key takeaway is this: Having the right people is only part of the solution. Company politics and the company culture must adapt so they can do their jobs. Triumphing over internal obstacles requires relentless focus and commitment, but moving into the Enlightened Age of Data is well worth the effort.

Data Strategy

When people ask me questions about the data hairball, I usually respond by explaining that it's one of those good news/bad news scenarios. First, there's the bad news: Untangling the data hairball won't be easy, or something you can do overnight. It is a journey that takes time—months and even years, to be honest. But, there's good news, too: Every step you take will improve insights and possibly even drive a quick win, providing the push you and your team need to keep going. What's more, savvy business leaders *are* beginning to tackle the data hairball. They're unraveling the complications and harnessing the power of new data-driven marketing strategies—best of all, we can learn from their success.

Here's a case in point: Many companies are appointing vice presidents of customer relationships or customer experience to develop what I call a master data strategy. Armed with this roadmap, these marketing pros are working across their organizations to improve the data management process, including data collection, storage, access, and application. In order to be successful, a master data strategy must consider all marketing processes, from planning to content development and execution.

How can their best practices impact your situation, and where should *your* company start? The following eight-point plan has worked well for large, multinational Fortune 100 organizations and high-growth companies as they create their data strategies. Keep in mind that while the size and scope of these organizations may differ from yours, you can easily adapt these guidelines to create your own path to change.

1. **Define the vision.** What customer experience do you want to deliver? Research the customer journey as it is now. Then, paint a picture of the future. How will you deliver on your promises and delight your customers? Include the details about how to make the vision a reality, and sketch out the steps to get there.

2. **Outline the questions you need to answer.** As Hayzlett's experience at Kodak showed, you need to know which business questions you want the data (and the team) to answer. Too many projects end in disappointment because they fail to keep the outcome in mind. If you aren't sure what questions to ask, conducting a discovery session with all the key stakeholders can help them bubble up organically.

3. **Assign the right team with the right sponsorship.** Make sure you bring together people who get it. As a *Harvard Business Review* article elegantly puts it, "Data gives you the *what*, but humans know the *why*."[3] The team you build needs to be multileveled, meaning you need to have CMO and CIO sponsorship to mow down obstacles, and you also need other executives like presidents, general managers, and chief operating officers to help. It will take senior-executive alignment and support to correctly implement your data strategy (and get it done sooner rather than later). Plus, you'll need the team to reach deep into the organization, across multiple departments and geographies. One more consideration: Everyone involved needs to be willing to challenge the status quo as needed.

4. **Identify the data requirements.** In this phase, you will find data you need that you don't currently capture. Be certain you understand what types of data you'll need to drive the desired customer experience, and to keep your team on track, don't lose sight of the vision and questions you defined in steps one and two. Look at the data you can currently access, and then map your future needs as they relate to your present abilities. This will reveal gaps in your current data program that you will need to address going forward.

5. **Find the source of the data you need.** You'll need to take inventory of what data exists and where. Make sure you look across the entire enterprise—this is where the CIO's support can be extremely helpful. Who knows? Other departments, such as research and development (R&D), customer support, inventory management, and business operations, may actually be collecting and storing the data you need. Add this information to the map you established in step four, then examine the remaining gaps and determine what additional data you need to collect.

6. **Identify and ready the single source of truth.** To manage the data across the enterprise—and to create and build an ongoing system to collect, access, and utilize it—you will want to work with your IT

team to build a storage destination with unified data collection and analytical capabilities. Most organizations typically use a combination of technologies to achieve a single source of verified data—what I like to call *the truth*. These enabling systems usually include a data model or organizational structure, an enterprise data warehouse to provide a single repository for organizational data, a big data analytics discovery platform that collects structured and unstructured data for analysis and insights, and a master data-management solution to build a single source of customer information to be used as the so-called *golden record*. With the game plan for the single source of truth in hand, your team will need to prepare and implement the architecture to support the next step.

7. **Consolidate, integrate, and iterate your data.** Once you have a *single source of the truth*, you need to populate it by bringing all the data together. Begin by consolidating and integrating the data to inform strategy, campaigns, and initiatives to elevate the customer experience. Complete the process of unraveling this part of the data hairball by devising *new* collection processes to use going forward, and add governance policies based on what you learn.

8. **Test, expand, and evolve.** You will want to measure and assess your progress. Start by answering the business questions developed in step two, and verify they are indeed the right questions. Then, test the data to ensure you have the right information to answer the questions and confirm the data's validity. This milestone can deliver some quick wins and identify landmines that need to be addressed before going any further. Chart out crucial points on your journey where more data will be available to improve a customer interaction or campaign, and then test those as well. This iterative approach will improve results and build confidence in the data.

Develop your data strategy step by step, and be sure to include small-scale, pilot projects. If you do, you'll be taking action as you learn with relatively low risk.

Discovering Big Data

The *one* question every C-level executive wants to know is where to start to collect and gather big data insights. My best advice: Start small.

In a 2012 *Harvard Business Review* blog, Bill Franks, the Chief Analytics Officer for Teradata Corporation and a longtime data-analysis expert, advises business professionals to rethink their traditional approaches before beginning any big data projects. Franks says most organizations typically start projects after an executive (often the CMO) realizes the company is missing out on opportunities in data. What follows is an exhaustive and time-consuming process by a cross-functional marketing and IT team to "specify and scope the precise insights to be pursued and the associated analytics to get them."[4] This work effort grows into a complex and time-consuming IT project to begin capturing and applying the data. Then, once other analytical experts in the company get their hands on the data, they start to poke holes in the approach, which undermines the team's efforts. This lack of credibility spawns another IT project, and so on and so on.

Sound familiar?

Franks says that what works for traditional data projects just won't work for big data initiatives, where the territory is new, and too many facts are unknown. This is especially true for marketing, where there have likely already been issues navigating and mastering many traditional data projects.

"My best advice is to start small. Define a few relatively simple analytics that won't take much time or data to run," Franks explains. "For example, an online retailer might start by identifying what products each customer viewed so that the company can send a follow-up offer if they don't purchase. A few intuitive examples like this allow the organization to see what the data can do."

Testing is an important element of this approach. Testing, as mentioned in the eight steps outlined above, can be used to explore what benefits analytics could provide to the business.

Franks also advises that teams maintain a strong focus. For instance, tackle a big data marketing project with a set timeframe and a fixed scope to capture all the data for just one subset of your products. When you limit the amount of data for analysis, projects are easier to manage and results are easier to understand.

What about the analytics pros who want to take a look at your data? As soon as you're ready, Franks says you should "turn them loose."

"Remember, they're used to dealing with raw data in an unfriendly format. They can zero in on what they need and ignore the rest," he explains. "They can create test and control groups to whom they can send the follow-up offers, and then they can help analyze the results.

During this process, they'll also learn an awful lot about the data and how to make use of it. This kind of targeted prototyping is invaluable when it comes to identifying trouble and firming up a broader effort."

As you start small, begin by identifying a business outcome you want to achieve. Some CMOs may choose to start with a better understanding of the *golden path*, the omnichannel touch points that serve as the consumer's path to purchase, including everything from social media tweets to call-center interactions. Others may prioritize diving into the customer behavior events that are leading to churn or attrition, such as service calls and usage declines.

The business outcome you choose will shape the scope of your big data discovery project. As I discussed in Chapter 6, any pilot should be well defined; just because a project is small-scale doesn't mean it should be half-baked, and it doesn't mean it will be easy. Pilot projects are valuable because they let you test your data strategy's feasibility with fewer resources and less risk than larger big data projects. Experiment, test, and learn. The value gained from even a small pilot project may surprise you!

To see how pilot projects can help move your efforts forward, take a look at how a based telecommunications firm is using data insights to find new ways to combat customer churn.

Big Data Insights Combat Churn for US Telecommunications Provider

As the telecom market reaches saturation, customer retention is an issue of utmost importance for companies in the mobile market, and one large service provider leveraged big data to battle this churn. The company conducted a pilot discovery project focusing on big data analytics to identify trigger points that lead to a customer canceling a mobile plan. One trigger point the company investigated was the customer support line. Since customers are often disgruntled when they call the customer support line of any organization, these interactions are a natural place to look for clues about why a customer might defect.

At first, it may seem that the easiest and most logical approach would be to ask customer service representatives to identify at-risk customers after talking with them. However, the general status of "likely to leave" does little to help improve the customer experience and save the relationship since it does not describe what is behind a customer's frustration.

Since the company's goal was to improve the customer experience, it made sense to identify what types of situations and problems precede a customer's decision to cancel a plan. To analyze what these telltale behaviors could be, the data-analysis team examined customer numbers and call center representatives' notes, along with the outcome (in this case whether the customer stayed or left). By performing sentiment analysis on the notes from the call, looking at a timeline of key events (e.g., purchasing a phone, changing a plan), and determining types of problems customers were having, this telecommunications company identified the behavior patterns that indicate defection risk.

As you can see, it pays to keep projects focused on a business result related to the desired customer experience. Don't ever try to tackle your entire data hairball in a single project or all at once. As a *Harvard Business Review* blog article on data scientists recommends, "Look only for data that affect your organization's key metrics."[5] By following this tip, you'll concentrate on the big data projects that answer questions directly affecting your key performance indicators (KPIs), and you'll provide measureable value for your company and your customer experience.

While the term *data hairball* may not evoke a pleasant initial reaction, it does grab an audience's attention. (In fact, I nearly used *Hairball* as the title for this book because the complicated process of untangling the data mess deserves to be front and center.) Everyone in the C-suite needs to recognize the dire need to unravel this jumble, and the sooner, the better. In order to maintain a competitive advantage, companies must institute a master data strategy that will help them uncover actionable insights, improve the customer experience, and accelerate revenue growth.

KEY TERMS

Data strategy: A roadmap to help you unravel the data hairball. Once you're armed with a data strategy, you can work across your organizations to improve the process of collecting, storing, accessing, and applying data into all marketing processes, including planning, content development, and execution.

Data model: A visual map of the relationship between data and systems.

DOs AND DON'Ts

Optimize the talent around you. Build your data strategy team with those who have tackled and integrated data across the enterprise before. However, make sure they are willing and able to innovate and develop creative new ways of looking at the data.

Chart out a journey. It took time to create the hairball, and it will take time to untangle it, too. You can't solve the problem overnight, but you *can* take small, meaningful steps every day. By charting out your journey, you can make sure that each small step leads to a larger goal.

Get what you need to succeed. In addition to talent, you'll need the right partnerships, data, models, and tools to get the job done. Therefore, you'll need to build support within the C-suite, and work with business analysts and data scientists on both the strategy and the pilots to test and validate progress.

Think big, but start small. Thinking big applies to the entire process and organization, from mapping out the future vision—and using that to build excitement and support—to broadly looking across the enterprise and your channels for the data that you need. However, big projects get complicated, and big data marketing is new territory, so, start small with a defined, well-understood project. Involve analytics professionals early so their expertise can help you understand and leverage what you learn to gain big value from small projects.

Don't pretend the problem will solve itself. Big data is here to stay, and so is the world of data-driven marketing. You need to start putting data to work for you now, as big data will continue to accumulate and enlarge the hairball.

Don't be afraid to ask for help. Great leaders realize they don't know it all. Although it may seem counterintuitive at first, knowing when to ask for help is a strength, not a weakness. Once you have the help you need, you can focus on innovation and leadership.

(continued)

(*continued*)

Don't feel overwhelmed by the sheer size of your data hairball. If you can focus on just one strand, you may realize that your pilot project gives you the experience and knowledge to unravel the next strand. Keep unraveling the knots, project by project, and it won't be long before you'll notice that your data hairball has shrunk considerably.

Don't start with trying to unravel all the data you have. Rather, begin by identifying the data you'll need for the immediate projects that actually have an impact on critical areas of your business. Those are the projects that will add value. And, be prepared: There will be times when you'll feel like you're adding to the data hairball. Don't worry. Even if you can't use it right away, you will want to collect and store this data for future use.

I was recently asked at a CMO Insights event what data is important and what is not. The truth is this: You never know. Now that the cost of data storage has dropped, you may not even have to make a choice. For instance, Hadoop offers an open-source platform that integrates in with data-warehousing and discovery platforms to store large data sets without huge financial burden. After you gain experience from your first few pilot projects, you can put processes and policies in place to ensure that the data is properly inventoried and stored as you collect it going forward.

9

Step Four

Make Metrics Your Mantra

Source: © Teradata 2013

Let's take a minute for a brief recap. As a smart business leader, you know it's time for your company to start taking advantage of data-driven marketing and big-data insights. So, you've opted to follow my five-step plan:

1. You've established a strategy.
2. You're tearing down silos.
3. You're working with your team to unravel the data hairball.

Along the way you've painted a clear vision for marketing's role in the company, and you've formed an alliance with the CIO. So what's next on your to-do list?

Your next step is to start *proving* that all these efforts are actually adding value to the business. You can do this by maintaining transparency with your data and processes, and by ensuring accountability across the marketing organization. That may sound like a tall order—and it is–but once again, you'll find it's all feasible if you tackle it using a step-by-step approach.

How do you demonstrate that marketing contributes value to the business? You use metrics to measure your progress. You and your team need to track conversations and engagement for every email campaign. You need to measure the return that every media buy brought to the bottom line of the business. Every year, you need to show precisely how you and your team are improving marketing's effectiveness and efficiency. Metrics, metrics, metrics. As I'm always telling my team, "Marketers, you need to make metrics your mantra."

Use Metrics to Measure Outcomes

I realize this book is devoted to big data marketing (and I hope I've convinced you there's good reason for that focus). However, I must provide a word of caution: Please don't make the mistake of letting the data consume you and distract you from the bigger picture. Some marketers are now so mesmerized with data that they have become completely engrossed in its tactical management, only to lose sight of the all important outcomes. They're tucked away, concentrating on identifying, organizing, and categorizing the data, but they never actually get around to leveraging it.

I recently met with a large technology company that serves as a good example of this phenomenon. Marketers at this company bragged about the volume of digital data they collected about their customers, but when I inquired how they were integrating this data with other information across the enterprise and with third party data providers they didn't have an answer. Instead, they asked me for best practices on how others are handling data management and integration.

To help you maintain the proper perspective and steer clear of the tactical data trap, make sure teams throughout your organization broadly assess the customer journey and can link metrics back to it. Then, once you start measuring impact on outcomes, you'll be able to identify gaps between the data and your business objectives. And don't forget the added bonus: All this increased accountability will make your marketing organization more valued within the company.

On the bright side, I find that the vast majority of marketers have begun to measure at least a few fundamental metrics, and most are now acclimated to reporting on campaign results and digital conversations. However, many are still reluctant to fully embrace this new world of data-driven marketing and the deeper measurement and keen scrutiny of outcomes it requires. The skepticism seems rooted in fear: fear about transparency, fear about job security, and fear about lacking the skills required to understand and communicate the metrics. To put it another way, marketers must go beyond basic measuring. We must pursue rigorous data analysis to gain insight into how to drive more sales, improve customer satisfaction, and strengthen marketing.

"It's not always about coming up with new ideas and being overly creative and oriented toward just trying new stuff," says Gautam Bose, General Manager of Customer Analytics and Research for National Australia Bank (NAB). "Use all the tools at hand to be more response- and results-oriented so resources can be reallocated to where they will make the greatest impact."[1]

As I mentioned above, some marketers are anxious about making this transition; they're just not accustomed to this level of examination. One CMO of a large well-established financial services institution confessed to me that her team was "nervous." They had endured several organizational realignments and therefore saw metrics as a negative tool senior management could use to "manage" marketers right out of their jobs. An anecdote like this underscores the work we have to do to help our organizations and our talent becomes more comfortable with metrics.

Others marketers seem convinced that embracing metrics is not even possible; they're certain modern marketing practices have grown too complicated and unwieldy. Believe me, I know the feeling.

Lessons Learned from Cost per Lead

As I mentioned in Chapter 5, when I first started as CMO of Aprimo (now Teradata Applications), I developed and achieved alignment on the five-prong scorecard to report marketing's contributions and value. The scorecard measured demand, customer satisfaction and retention, sales productivity, market category leadership, and overall effectiveness of the marketing organization. Each of these five metrics mapped back to our overall business objectives and represented the work marketing accomplished to grow revenue, brand awareness, and customer loyalty. In addition to these metrics, I also aspired to track the return on marketing investment (ROMI) in that first year. I wanted to prove to the C-suite that our marketing team served as a strategic growth driver of our business, but it didn't take me long to realize that goal was overly ambitious. Yes, we had an integrated marketing platform to help us manage planning, spend, and campaign execution. And, yes we had operational analytics. But we were missing measurements that tracked cross-channel interactions and pegged them against our total spend.

Back then, as a high-growth company, we didn't rigorously apply those cross-channel attributions to resource allocation. So, while my goal to track ROMI was certainly aspirational, we weren't prepared to take such a big bite of the apple.

I reconnoitered and, as a team, we decided to take a different tack. We continued working to improve our cross-channel campaign measurement, but concurrently, we began to seek out low-hanging fruit, such as cost per lead (a sensible choice for any business-to-business (B2B) marketing organization starting the journey to measure outcomes). Of course, cost per lead is just one data point in overall ROMI, but it was key for us to track it so we could learn the requirements, processes, and steps involved in tracking a much larger view of our marketing effectiveness.

Within a few months, we were able to report our results at the board level, and from there, we began adjusting and optimizing spend, even as we paved the path for more metrics and a broader analysis of ROMI. Our approach using cost per lead as an incremental step is similar to how other business leaders tackle problems using pilot projects—they learn, test, and evolve over time. This journey taught me that metrics and measurement could be successfully implemented if you start with a big vision and then execute with small, short-term goals. Once you establish credibility and momentum, you can align metrics across the marketing organization and the entire enterprise and achieve larger, broad-based objectives.

Part I: The ROI versus ROMI Debate

Incremental steps, like accounting for cost per lead, move you one step closer toward that elusive measurement of every marketing dollar. But, you should be aware that there's disagreement about whether this is the best approach. Some industry thought leaders are convinced that most companies cannot measure every dollar they spend. In fact, Jim Lenskold, the CEO of the Lenskold Group and a leading industry expert on marketing measurement, says the focus of the C-suite should be on *improving* return on investment, rather than *proving* return on investment. According to Lenskold, it's better to measure and act on select metrics than to attempt to measure everything for reporting purposes.[2]

Either way, determining exactly what and how to measure remains problematic for many companies—and sometimes, those debates are decades old. The conversation about marketing spend metrics started back in 1964 with Kristian Palda's *The Measurement of Cumulative Advertising Effects*,[3] but it didn't truly gain steam until the 1990s, when marketers began trying to fully understand and measure ROMI. In late 1991, Gary Lilien, Philip Kotler, and K.Sridhar Moorthy published a book, *Marketing Models*, which forged an approach of tracking marketing effectiveness and performance; however, more than a decade later, there's still plenty of confusion to go around.[4]

Let's start with a few of the basic terms and concepts.

Return on Investment (ROI) versus Return on Marketing Investment

The two terms are ever so similar, but how you use them can impact interpretation and alignment. Finance is accustomed to ROI and has models to determine it for key investments. However, some marketing academics and business professionals point out that ROI is built to measure to a one-time capital investment, such as adding a new facility or funding a major corporate purchase. Therefore, they argue that ROI may not be the right term or the right calculation for measuring marketing spend.

It's a good point. Does looking at a one-time marketing spend and its return best translate the value of marketing?

Other thought leaders take the opposing view. For example, Lenskold considers ROI to be the most credible approach for marketing since it is a model financial professionals understand. Since 1997, Lenskold has worked to offer one of the most comprehensive and innovative approaches to applying marketing measurability techniques and tools to plan, measure, and optimize marketing strategies toward maximum profitability, and in 2011, my team and I collaborated with him on a white paper titled, "The CMO Guide to Marketing ROI."[5] Here's an excerpt:

> Marketing's primary objective is to generate more profits with its existing resources, which is accomplished by improving both effectiveness and efficiency. The first step to managing marketing profitability is to quantify the expected outcomes from the marketing investment being planned. This means running the numbers for the budget and offering expenses against the expected incremental sales and financial contribution.
>
> Quantifying the stages of the purchase funnel—from initial target audience reached, to changes in customer perceptions and behaviors, and ultimately to customer purchase decisions—can help you provide a better view of how marketing influences financial outcomes. Quantifying the impact also shows where a marketing program may be dependent on other marketing or sales initiatives to drive a conversion (such as leads passed to the sales organization or customers motivated to enter a retail store before purchasing).

Figure 9.1 shows a simple formula to calculate the value of marketing and to align the approach with the finance organization.

Regarding the calculations, Lenskold says:

> . . . accurate ROI calculations, regardless of how basic or advanced, are a critical starting point. This doesn't mean you'll have hard data for every aspect of your marketing spend; many marketing teams will begin with rough assumptions for a handful of input values while working toward more detailed and reliable values from analytics and measurements. The simplest version of a marketing ROI calculation must include the incremental profit, which is driven by the incremental sales generated, the revenue per sale, and the gross margin percent, and the marketing expense.

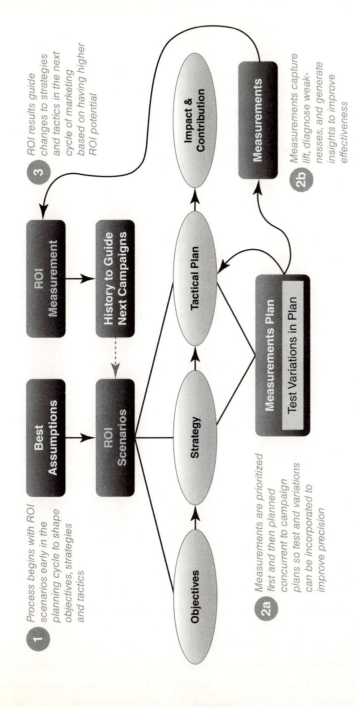

FIGURE 9.1 Marketing ROI Management Process

Source: Jim Lenskold White paper. Recreated and reprinted with permission from "The CMO Guide to Marketing ROI" © 2010.

Part II: The ROI versus ROMMI Debate

Are you ready to dive in even deeper? The ROI versus ROMI debate isn't the only one brewing. Dominique Hanssens, Bud Knapp Distinguished Professor of Marketing at the UCLA Anderson School of Management and co-founder of marketing analytics firm MarketShare, cautions against the blind use of marketing ROI as a performance metric because he believes it is highly dependent on the brand's spending level. Indeed, most marketing spending is subject to diminishing returns to scale, so the more you spend, the lower the ROI, all else equal. As Hanssens sees it, using ROI could lead to brands underinvesting in marketing. He suggests that executives should focus on the return on *marginal (or incremental)* marketing investment (ROMMI), which centers on the question "What is the return on, for example, the last $1,000 spent on each marketing activity?" With this model, a company has reached its maximum profit when the ROMMI is equal to zero. Positive ROMMI indicates that more resources could be allocated, and negative ROMMI indicates overspending. Hanssens's approach adapts basic ROI thinking for marketing to align a brand's revenue and profit aspirations.

Metrics Are the Cornerstone of Accountability

Marketers are under more pressure than ever before to be accountable, and while there's no doubt they're rising to the occasion, many CMOs I speak with get downright testy when they express their concerns about this trend. Specifically, they're worried that marketing is becoming overly metrics driven. Will marketers forget there is as much an *art* to marketing as there is science? These CMOs are aware that one of their top priorities in managing brands is to marry instinct with data, and they're concerned that measurement and data are increasingly overshadowing the more creative side of marketing. I often find myself explaining that data-driven marketing isn't about taking the art out of marketing; rather, it's a way for marketers to achieve balance and gain more credibility and strategic insights. Plus, we have the benefit of today's digital marketing tools that help us visualize, automate, and understand the information to drive greater accountability.

One U.S.-based, household-name consumer electronics company with both a B2B and a business-to-consumer (B2C) division uses integrated marketing management (IMM) solutions to help marketing managers across multiple business units and geographic locations create measurable lead-nurturing, event management, dialog management, and email marketing.

By tracking marketing spend and measuring results across multiple business units and channels, the marketing team was able to deliver ROI metrics and clear business benefits, including:

- Better targeting, message consistency, and tracking for email marketing campaigns, which has improved performance against key metrics by more than 200 percent and increased cross-selling performance.
- More efficient workflow and access to shared campaign design and creative assets, which has improved efficiency with reduced expense.
- Financial tracking of marketing spend by activity, which has resulted in proactive management of marketing.
- More consistent communication of marketing initiatives across the organization, which has resulted in improved effectiveness and better coordination across multiple initiatives.

Leading marketing organizations now routinely utilize performance dashboards (like the one in Figure 9.2) and work to align those measures

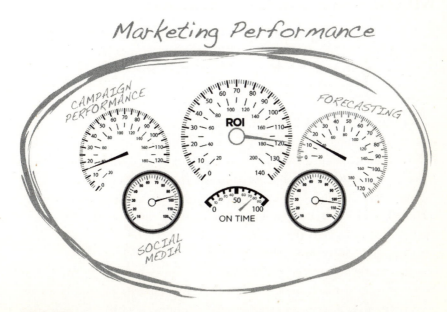

FIGURE 9.2   Conceptual Marketing Performance Dashboard

Source: © Teradata 2013

across the organization. They've learned to accept nothing less than a ruthless analysis of the money they're spending. They know that in order to understand the value of any campaign, marketers need to identify, track, evaluate, and then refine the metrics that provide the most insight.

Metrics Improve Buy-In and Alignment

In addition to providing accountability, metrics strengthen organization-wide buy-in and alignment. As a B2B marketer, I've long seen the disconnect that exists between most marketing and sales organizations. Others are well aware of it, but most companies do little to fix the problem. In fact, some firms just view this baseline disagreement and uncooperative behavior as a fact of life. They think of sales and marketing as stubborn siblings who are always going to have differences of opinions. Fortunately, metrics can help these "family members" get along.

After all, have you ever stopped to realize how much this misalignment is costing you? According to B2B marketing strategist, speaker, and blogger Christine Crandell:[6]

- As many as 80 percent of B2B leads passed on to sales are dropped.
- A staggering 90 percent of marketing collateral goes unused, and
- The total cost of winning a net new enterprise customer via direct sales averages about $500,000.

What's more, Crandell estimates that the vast majority (80 percent) of enterprise technology deals won are not influenced by marketing at all. Who's at fault? Both departments. Misalignment not only results in lost revenue, but it also has contributed to enterprise sales cycles doubling in the past decade. That puts even more pressure on marketing to produce qualified leads at a time when more than 65 percent of CEOs have openly communicated their lack of faith in marketing's value. Crandell explains that, historically, the alignment problem was attributed to the fact that marketing and sales each have their own charters, planning time horizons, and compensation models. The real culprits of misalignment, according to Crandell, are marketing's disconnect with the company's near- and long-term financial realities and its lack of understanding how the customer journey has fundamentally changed. In other words, in many ways, marketing has been flying blind.

Reasons for Misalignment

John Petralia, Head of Global Operations at Bloomberg and former marketing executive at Iron Mountain and Xerox, has built a successful career driving value to his company through strategic marketing alignment. In addition to his day job running global marketing operations for Bloomberg, a multinational mass media firm based in New York City, he speaks to marketing executives across the country to help them understand how to align marketing for strategic business contributions. At a 2013 Marketing Science Institute (MSI) conference, Petralia cited the following issues as core reasons for misalignment:[7]

- **Lexicon:** Marketing uses words like *reach*, *clicks*, and *brand awareness*, whereas sales is thinking about *pipeline*, *conversions of leads*, and *quotas*. It isn't uncommon for sales or other business functions to think that marketing is trying to pull the wool over their eyes when they use these terms because often, the rest of the organization doesn't understand what the marketers are trying to convey. Take the pulse of your own organization. Is your team using marketing terms that are not clearly understood? Ask your peers what they see and hear. As I discussed in Chapter 4, if this is a problem it is easy to rectify by starting every conversation with clear definitions and working to adopt common definitions. It is also helpful to eradicate confusing terms and use more common monikers instead. For example, consider eliminating the term *brand* internally when it is viewed tactically by the broader organization. You might also want to avoid using terms like *value propositions*, or *promise*. Every organization is different, but a universal agreement of the meaning of key terms really matters.
- **Lack of understanding:** Petralia, a veteran marketing executive, believes that too often marketing doesn't have a solid appreciation of what sales does—and this creates a gap that can be hard to bridge. He recommends marketing "take a walk in sales' shoes," or even the customer's if there is no direct sales channel. I've seen this same dynamic and have championed shadow programs that place the marketing team

in the field with key sales leaders and professionals to observe, learn, and develop a stronger relationship. Invariably when the marketing team returns, projects to help sales get prioritized and the relationship improves. It doesn't have to be complicated or difficult to execute this kind of shadow program.

- **Aligning to the customer/buyer experience**: Petralia counsels, "We must stop thinking of it as a *selling cycle*, and think more of it as a *buying* cycle." That shift in thinking will prompt marketing and sales to co-develop new ways to collaborate to get the right content in front of prospects and to prioritize the marketing assets and deliverables so they jointly contribute to revenue.

- **Shared business objectives**: I've already discussed how marketing leadership must work together to outline overall shared objectives and then map their organization's metrics. Petralia also sees this as a critical step to alignment and success. "Too often companies set metrics in isolation only to find later that no one else thought these were essential to the business," warns Petralia. The senior marketing leadership must sit down with their peers and align on the metrics they will track, the metrics they require from other organizations, the cadence, and the communication plan. This critical step ensures that the metrics marketing tracks are value-added measures. It also enables marketing to engage with other teams to get help when data lies outside the traditional walls of the department.

The marketing and sales groups at Teradata Applications aligned to build a true partnership by implementing shared metrics, transparency, and common definitions. We sent team members out into the field and observed sales, and this experience helped our marketers develop an understanding of precisely where the misalignments were. While sales was working from the perspective of moving prospects and customers through the steps of the *sales process*, marketing was creating tools and marketing based on the stages of the customer *buying cycle*. This simple observation—and knowing where we had to close the gap—led to a more aligned buying cycle. To help foster adoption, we developed a simple graphic we now use in sales training that conveys how the steps of the sales process line up to the stages of the customer buying cycle. By aligning our departments' definitions, sales now has a better understanding of when they should use the tools marketing has provided for them targeting various points of the customer buying cycle.

The marketing and sales groups worked together to develop a closed-loop view, which they then used to go to the C-suite for funding. We aligned on the sales funnel to show that marketing contributed and drove better than 65 percent of pipeline. Metrics kept us true to our objectives and provided results we could all celebrate and rally behind as we continued improving.

I also suggest marketing leaders collaborate with chief financial officers (CFOs) on the process to connect marketing spend to financial data. Securing CFO and COO buy-in ensures the data has integrity and is linked to the right financial information. Moreover, aligning across the organization as you measure, report, and run the business of marketing with metrics helps the C-suite gain confidence in the measurements.

Metrics. Accountability. Value. Proofpoints. These are commonly on the list of what C-level executives want marketing to improve. And yes, even though digital interactions are easier to measure, marketers still have to do the heavy lifting. We have to develop a holistic view of marketing. We have to work to understand the best way to measure those initiatives and activities. And we have to guarantee the entire organization understands and sees values in the metrics we bring back. Just like other elements of big data marketing, establishing metrics can be a daunting task—but it's one that's well worth the effort. Aligned metrics will provide you with more confidence in decisions, more granularity about what to focus on, and a more credible function in the end.

KEY TERMS

Return on Investment (ROI): There is no doubt that virtually all business professionals use ROI all the time, and marketers are using it more and more, too. To build credibility, it's critical that marketing ROI follow the same ROI definition used by finance. The best definition I found describes ROI as a ratio comparing the incremental profit generated in excess of the original marketing investment to the marketing investment. The ratio is positive when marketing generates more profit than the cost and

(continued)

(*continued*)

negative when the marketing investment is not fully recovered. The formula is:

$$\text{Return on Investment} = \text{Net Profit/Investment}$$
$$= (\text{Profit from incremental sales}$$
$$- \text{Marketing Investment})/$$
$$\text{Marketing Investment}$$

Return on Marginal Marketing Investment (ROMMI, or sometimes ROMI^2): This is one approach to taking a longer-term look at return on spend and its return to the business. ROMMI is the adaptation of the return on marginal investment metric so it's specific to marketing.

Marketing performance dashboard: An aggregation of key metrics across marketing, as defined by an organization and its leadership, that is displayed in a single view. Often called a scorecard, report card, or marketing dashboard, these tools are essential for checking the health of programs and efforts, and they are needed to report back to board and other C-level executives. Common metrics include spend, campaign results, cost per program, and demand generation status, just to name a few.

Cost per lead: One of the leading analyst firms tracking B2B is SiriusDecisions, so I sought out their definition in helping explain this metric. SiriusDecisions defines marketing cost per lead as "the annual marketing campaign program cost plus internal teleprospecting staffing costs divided by the resulting number of marketing leads."[8]

DOs AND DON'Ts

Equip yourself with the right tools. Today's technologies allow you to track your way toward revenue goals, get instant visibility into spending and campaign ROI, know where you stand on customer satisfaction measures or market share growth (and virtually any other metric you need), and adjust your plans accordingly.

Focus on results. The C-suite won't be impressed with the number of website clicks, Twitter followers, or Facebook "likes." Executives want *results*. They don't want to look at metrics for metrics' sake. So use metrics that demonstrate marketing's contribution to the company's objectives, such as ROMI or the number of marketing-qualified leads, to give them what they want.

Build your organizational models based on your strategy. It is essential to keep your strategy in mind. Sure, it will shift over time, but it must always be tied to accountability. Years ago, I always measured everything my team did against what others did. I compared and contrasted programs. I researched and modeled my marketing organization's structure with what was happening at other companies. I would scratch my head and feel frustrated when our results didn't measure up. Of course, it makes sense to understand and immerse ourselves in our industry's best practices during times of high change and transformation. But, it is ultimately up to us in this Enlightened Age of Data to define the *next practices* for our organizations. What works for others may not work for your organization or company, and it is essential for you to develop a core set of measures that tie to *your* customers' buying journey and marketing's role in supporting and driving your buying cycle. You'll also need to establish metrics that demonstrate prudent and effective use of the marketing budget—one of the biggest assets of most companies.

Don't get lost in data. Work with your peers, your CEO, and your team to understand what metrics matter and which outcomes will drive true value to revenue and customer retention. Then, work to measure broadly and deeply. Most importantly, take action on the insights gained from the metrics to optimize your marketing.

(continued)

(*continued*)

Don't get discouraged. With the many steps involved, it can be a real challenge for leaders to persevere on their journey to establish a data-driven marketing organization. Keep the vision in your sights, but don't lose faith that each step along the way, from accessing new data that can improve measurement, to aligning groups around *what* to measure, is a victory. Even small steps, if missed, can derail you, so tackling them as you go will help you achieve your ultimate objective. Remember: Small victories add up to winning the war.

10

Step Five

Process Is the New Black

Source: © Teradata 2013

Marketers aren't generally the type to consider business processes to be sexy. Who wants to waste time with *process*—a term defined as "a series of logically related tasks performed to produce a defined set of results"[1]—when they could be focusing on more exciting and strategic initiatives, like the next great creative campaign or a killer product launch?

However, I believe that it's time for a shift in that mindset. In this chapter, I'm going to prove that process *is* sexy. I'll show why process is the new black, and I'll explain that, without process, your marketing efforts to collect and analyze big data will fall short of expectations, every single time. Your company simply *cannot* move from the Dark Ages into the Enlightened Age of Data without having the proper processes in place.

Now, before we continue this discussion, let's make sure we're all on the same page. When I talk about today's marketing processes, I'm not talking about the old-fashioned way of doing business—you know, the way a marketer used to fill out a hard-copy job starter form to initiate a marketing project, cram that into a color-coded folder with a stack of other papers, and then walk it all to and fro to track down creative review and approvals. No, I'm not talking about that kind of process. By process, I mean modern, purpose-built marketing activities made possible by advances in marketing technology and automation. Today's processes are sleek and sophisticated. They're what enable marketers to regain control of the modern marketing environment.

Process Is One of Marketing's New Four P's

Philip Kotler's famous book covering the 4 P's of Marketing—product, price, placement, and promotion—have aptly served as the basic roadmap of marketing organizations since the 1960s.[2] However, given all that's changed in marketing, it's time for the classic 4 P's to evolve. I don't believe the 4 P's are dead, as others have suggested; they simply need an update. Kotler himself has expanded his quartet to now include a fifth P, purpose. But, I'd like to see even more of an evolution—one that includes yet another *process*.

In 2012, industry thought-leader and Gartner Vice President of Research, Kim Collins, published a paper entitled, "The New Four Ps of Marketing." In it, she advises modern businesses to rethink marketing functions based on a fresh, updated set of P's: people, processes, performance, and profit—and she hit the nail on the head. In brief, marketers need to:

1. Align people and processes across marketing, both internally and externally, to coordinate the entire ecosystem.

2. Improve marketing performance and measurements.
3. Transform marketing to a profit center.

She writes:

Aligning people for collaboration and knowledge sharing is important, but documenting and automating processes is essential to ensuring effective and efficient alignment. As the complexity of marketing increases, process becomes [necessary] to align the appropriate people with the right marketing activities, to achieve faster times to market, to allocate human resources effectively and to perform closed-loop marketing. Without well-defined processes for marketing, it is impossible to manage the complexity, measure marketing outcomes and plan strategically.[3]

Integrated Marketing Processes Accelerate Results

Collins also mentions integrated marketing management (IMM), an approach that, in her words, "represents the business strategy, process automation and technologies required to integrate people, processes and technologies across the marketing ecosystem."[4]

I've been a proponent of IMM ever since I did research with business-to-business (B2B) marketing services agency Mobium to identify the top opportunities for our brand. A majority of the 100-plus marketers we surveyed globally cited they "craved realizing the vision" of integrating their marketing functions. But keep in mind: Today's IMM is not the "integrated marketing" we've seen over the past 15 years. It's not just a unified look and feel, and a consistent, aligned message. Rather, today's IMM stands for the *true* integration of marketing: integrating data, processes, campaigns, channels, and insights. IMM software (or an IMM platform) is now a requirement for agile marketing processes. It's a must-have for companies that want to take action on the data they aggregate, and it's necessary to help eliminate the silos of data and the antiquated approach to marketing management. IMM is what will move your company from the Dark Ages into the Enlightened Age of Data.

The way I like to explain IMM is really quite simple. IMM comprises four key areas: marketing operations, customer interaction management, digital interactions, and marketing performance management. The figure at the beginning of the chapter shows how integrating helps unify and streamline the way the marketing department functions.

One of the cornerstones of IMM is marketing operations, or, as industry analyst Gartner calls it, "marketing resource management" (MRM), a combination of marketing talent dedicated to processes, metrics, and systems and the application of this talent to drive marketing effectiveness and efficiency. Large global brands have seen this as a key area to staff and automate, and the appetite is growing to invest in both the technology and the function marketing operations plays in driving value for enterprises today.

I tapped an industry expert, Jason Grice, Vice President of Solution Management at EMMcare, a leading marketing technology consulting firm, for his take on process. Grice cites that heavily regulated industries have always been ahead of the curve in valuing a defined, repeatable process. Not just for efficiency, but for transparency and governance. He considers the biggest challenge for most firms to be the technology learning curve, as marketing teams have not traditionally been technology-focused in marketing management. Grice sees marketing process management and automation technology as a key part of how marketing departments will succeed moving forward.

Integrated Processes Improve Responsiveness

The faith-based non-profit Focus on the Family has used integrated marketing processes to improve its go-to-market results. In one compelling example, Focus on the Family was able to capitalize on the Denver Broncos' 2012 National Football League (NFL) playoff victory and celebrity quarterback Tim Tebow's role in the win. As explained in one case study,[5] Tebow, a devout Christian and longtime promoter of the John 3:16 Bible passage, had starred in a Focus on the Family commercial in 2010. Then, in 2012, Tebow helped the Denver Broncos pull off an upset to advance in the NFL playoffs. During the game, Tebow threw the football for 316 yards, which correlates to the number of his favorite John passage. Both the media and US audiences went into a frenzy. Focus on the Family saw an opportunity and, by using marketing operations to streamline processes, the non-profit needed only three-and-a-half days to produce a national television ad campaign that ran during the NFL playoff game the following weekend.

The case study spells out the *why* behind marketing operations, with Focus on the Family as a proof point. "Marketing is moving toward more fast-paced, responsive, and interactive campaigns. Big Data, technology improvements, and advances in analytics enable marketers to make rapid decisions—but can they create, execute, and deliver campaigns just as quickly?" Brooke Borgias asks in the case study.

By focusing on more effective marketing operations, and improving its coordination and execution, Focus on the Family demonstrated that greater efficiency drives better marketing.

The Many Benefits of Integrated Processes

As marketers from Focus on the Family proved, integrating strategic marketing processes empowers organizations to align teams and improve responsiveness. Integration also helps convert raw data into the actionable insights that increase revenue. Once marketing teams implement defined processes and automate the science of marketing, they can:

- **Drive focus and early value.** Automation allows marketers to extract the most relevant information from the constant deluge of big data.
- **Build measurement *into* the plan.** You can't manage what you don't measure, and having processes in place helps develop metrics and benchmarks.
- **Improve agility.** Automated processes allow real-time decision making.
- **Accelerate time-to-market.** Old-fashioned, manual marketing is slow and ineffective. Today's streamlined processes simplify reviewing and eliminate bottlenecks.
- **Cut costs.** Having processes in place allows marketers to easily see what's working, and stop doing what isn't.
- **Show results.** Accountability is crucial. Defined, automated processes enable analytics to demonstrate ROI, even among cross-functional groups.

- **Collaborate.** Data that's been aggregated and analyzed is easier to communicate and share.
- **Innovate.** Automation creates the awareness required to optimize future campaigns.
- **Beef-up compliance.** A thoughtful system ensures that critical steps aren't missed or forgotten, and that all sign-offs are in place.

Honestly, the list could go on and on. When I'm asked to sum it up, I like to say this: Modern marketing processes are a way to simplify what *doesn't* differentiate your company (e.g., creative reviews, campaign execution, etc.), so you can then apply strategy to what *does* make you unique.

Concept to Campaign to Cash

Process is also a key driver in the adoption of IMM as workflows and automation allow a more holistic approach to critical marketing processes, such as planning, budgeting, and campaign execution. IMM also enables the integration of the macro business processes that help deliver a more comprehensive view of marketing management—and that new perspective is long overdue. Too many marketers still rely on email to manage and conduct creative reviews. Too many still manage annual budgeting and planning processes in complicated spreadsheets. Meanwhile, too few reap the benefits of improved insights provided by big data. In fact, according to a recent Teradata research study, 42 percent of marketers said their top obstacle to using data in decision making is lack of processes to integrate insights into decisions.[6] That needs to change. Compliance pressures in certain industries, especially financial services and pharmaceuticals, have accelerated the adoption and focus on process because of the need to document and archive approvals across multiple lines of business, including legal. The risk of fines and penalties for mistakes, such as improper labeling or failure to communicate sensitive information to required audiences in heavily regulated industries, is driving adoption and commitment to automated processes.

Fortunately, once systems are updated, the threat of penalties and process adoption quickly gives way to faster time to market and cost relief benefits. After suffering millions of dollars in fines, a global financial services company in the EU used integrated processes to transform its noncompliant marketing department. As a result, the firm saw an 80 percent improvement in time to market on marketing programs and materials to support launches and marketing promotional campaigns. In light of results like these, it's no surprise more and more marketers want to improve their departmental operations.

When I'm explaining IMM, I like to apply a macro business approach. It helps simplify the concept so chief marketing officers (CMOs) and their teams can visualize how processes can streamline the complex world of marketing. Borrowing from Business Process Management and other software firms that have crafted names to define this—I and several other CMOs like to think of this macro marketing process as "concept to campaign" and "campaign to cash"—or shortened even further to "concept to campaign to cash."

Concept to Campaign

Imagine a typical marketing business strategy cycle. It's usually bottom-up planning, done deep within the marketing organization, and it's usually cross-functional, so general managers, brand managers, and sales teams can align on growth, revenue goals, and the marketing required to support new initiatives.

Generally, planning generates more ideas than can be executed, so the next step is for the ideas to be reviewed and distilled into a prioritized plan that points back to business objectives. Once that plan is refined, it begins to evolve into cascading activities and creative assignments. Then, the creative review process launches with a creative brief that drives the work streams to develop ideas, often in collaboration with outside parties like agencies or contractors. From there, the plan must survive review and approval processes, and, in many industries, that includes legal and key stakeholders outside of marketing. Finally, as the creative process concludes, the campaign is ready to execute.

Campaign to Cash

As the creative review ends, the campaign process begins, marked by a readiness to execute outbound promotions, offers, and integrated outreach programs. Database marketers start applying the segmentation strategy that will complement the marketing strategy. Data is readied, and lists are created. Execution occurs across multiple channels, such as websites, call centers, email, and perhaps even traditional direct mail. (Yes, you read correctly. Direct mail continues to drive engagement for some products or brands.) The campaign then drives awareness and demand, and once a consumer or buyer expresses interest and purchases the item, the transaction can be traced to the revenue, or cash.

Connecting these two macro processes integrates the go-to-market processes for marketers and provides better visibility, better outcomes, and more effective marketing. Let's dive deeper into a company that applied programmatic process to improve its marketing effectiveness and business results.

Process Innovation at a Global IT Services Company

When the CMO of a global high-tech IT services company first stepped into his role a few years ago, he was faced with several significant challenges. The firm had grown rapidly through a series of acquisitions, and each entity brought under the company's master brand had its own marketing strategy and infrastructure. As a result, it was increasingly difficult to monitor and coordinate marketing activities across the global enterprise, and the CMO realized that, in order to move the company forward, he would have to spearhead an effort to centralize the execution and measurement of marketing while providing modern infrastructure and tools for the company's marketing teams and senior management worldwide.

The CMO's broad technology and engineering background, coupled with a technology-savvy marketing team, provided strong underpinnings to tackle this complex job. Everyone on the team understood that, to measure across the entire marketing organization by geography or campaign, they needed to integrate business processes and work streams, and then require all the systems and data from these traditionally disconnected functions to integrate and be measured.

To start, the company's marketing operations team identified five key metrics that could be aggregated, tracked, and reported by region and marketing campaign: marketing spend, responses, leads generated, prospect opportunities, and sales pipeline. Then, they established an overarching campaign-to-cash process that would use process and big data insights to integrate and streamline customer engagement and lead management, while delivering the data to measure results and identify areas for improvement. Figure 10.1 illustrates this campaign-to-cash process and, as you can see, it transcends the silos within marketing, and with a few tweaks, can be applied to any marketing department, regardless of whether its business-to-consumer (B2C) or business-to-business (B2B).

To deliver on an integrated marketing process and metrics, the IT service firm's marketing team consolidated fragmented marketing technology systems like stand-alone email, campaign management applications, and project management. They also instituted and embraced a consolidated, integrated marketing management approach to manage the overall department.

Over time, the campaign-to-cash strategy enabled the marketing team to achieve full visibility of more than 80 percent of the total marketing budget, and they have been able to link that spend to different initiatives, such as the type of message and product focus. In addition, improved visibility empowered the team to use analytics to shorten decision-cycle time from weeks to mere days. Now that the marketing team can make data-driven decisions quickly, they can continually target marketing funds to the most effective campaigns, optimizing both mix and spend. This concentration of marketing budget and resources has contributed directly to increasing the number of successful events, product launches, and marketing activities, which in turn have improved the company's brand awareness and supported growth in sales revenue.

The company's marketers aren't the only ones feeling the benefits. Having a single record of all consumer interactions has enabled the company to provide a better experience for its customers. For example, now that the marketing team can attribute web activities to known prospects, the company's marketers can build profiles for targeted communications that deliver more personalized and relevant messages. The consolidation of profile data has also eliminated the frustration customers felt when they were asked to answer the same question over and over again.

Interestingly, process innovation went even further than the campaign-to-cash process that drove marketing and sales alignment. The company realized that, as a data-driven marketing organization, it needed to be able to pivot campaigns, content, and even organizations based on big data insights.

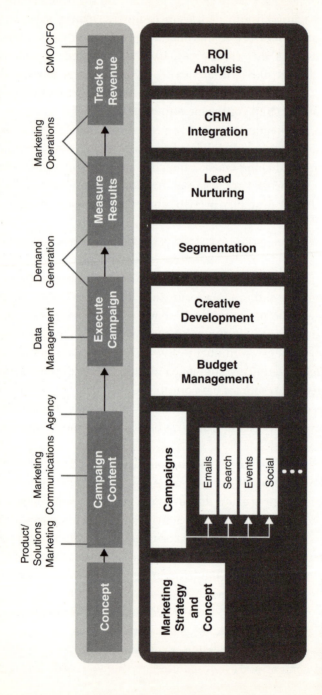

FIGURE 10.1   The Concept-to-Campaign-to-Cash Marketing Process

Source: © Teradata/Aprimo 2010

So, the company began using an agile product development methodology to implement the integrated marketing software that would support the macro and micro marketing processes needed to deliver value and results to the company. The CMO and his team established aggressive goals and, remarkably, they were able to deliver full value in just three months. The data—and the confidence—that these quick wins brought motivated the team to strive to drive even further change and alignment.

Agile Marketing

As underscored in the case study above, of all the benefits that *sexy*, updated marketing processes afford, one of the most important is improved agility. Marketing represents a rapidly shifting landscape, and organizations need to be more responsive and nimble so they can adjust and evolve to capitalize on all that's changing.

It's essential to be able to pivot to respond to market conditions, data insights, or organizational change, and move your marketing organization quickly and to flawless execution. Firms that are agile can pivot, and that's why I'm hearing the word *agile* applied to marketing more and more these days. Agile marketing, although still in its early days, is gaining momentum.

Of course, the term *agile* gained popularity in the high-tech product development world, and several companies now focus on agility to increase market responsiveness—a key asset in driving effective customer engagement.

I'm ending this chapter as I began it: by firmly asserting that process is the new black. Companies that want to move forward must jettison provisional management processes, ad hoc applications, and "taped-together" technologies, so they can better understand and interpret big data. When they do, internal teams won't be the only ones who reap the rewards; their stakeholders, shareholders, and customers will benefit, too. Building more silos and placing "band aids" on top of small wounds that later turn into bigger pains is dangerous and ultimately, does nothing. By contrast, implementing modern marketing processes improves collaboration and optimizes the efficiencies that are vital to success in today's multifaceted, fast-paced, and volatile marketing environment.

KEY TERMS

Pivot: to respond to market conditions, data insights, or organizational change and move your marketing organization quickly and to flawless execution. Firms that are agile are able to pivot, which allows them to take advantage of emerging opportunities.

Integrated Marketing Management (IMM): the integration of people, processes, data, technologies, and channels. IMM focuses on simplifying the complexity of data, processes, interaction channels, and insights and comprises four key areas: marketing operations, customer interaction management, digital interactions, and marketing performance management. IMM provides the tools needed to not only streamline internal workflow, but also to interact with customers and prospects in innovative and personalized ways across an ever-widening array of channels and platforms.

Agile marketing: a term adapted from applying iterative project and process management in software development. AgileMarketing.net has the best definition I've seen. It lists the values of agile as "responding to changes with a plan; leveraging testing and data over opinions and conventions; [executing] small, targeted experiments [instead of] big, time- and resource-consuming projects; collaborating over silos and hierarchy; and [embracing] engagement and transparency over posturing and politics."[7]

DOs AND DON'Ts

Use process to ramp up accountability. I've discovered that insisting on accountability from my team doesn't make me a dictator. In fact, it makes me *more* of a team player.

Accountability creates the feedback and dialogue required for clarity and collaboration. Insist on accountability, and your team will find: 1) their agendas have become less cluttered, because responsibilities are clearly outlined, and 2) healthy debate reveals better solutions.

Partner with IT. Have you noticed this theme runs through every chapter? You will need and *want* a robust collaboration with IT to help you address data gaps, develop a comprehensive strategy, and remove the channel silos that fragment data and dilute customer engagement.

Embrace integrated marketing with an IMM platform. Markets change, and so do marketing departments, strategies, and campaigns. To stay agile, you need to obliterate fractured systems that fragment data. Instead, you must unify core business applications to implement cross-functional and global processes, and have checks and balances in place to measure the impact.

Don't rest on your laurels. Reevaluate your processes periodically. You need to keep pace with today's changing marketplace.

Don't be afraid to get dirty. Dig in. Question the existing tools and systems and focus on consolidating technologies, channels, and data. Define processes and determine what analytics are required for the individual customer view, as well as for overall customer and operational performance analytics.

IV

Realizing the Value of Big Data Marketing

11 Drive Value through Relevant Marketing

A t its core, big data marketing centers on one thing and one thing only: driving value by engaging customers more effectively. That may sound straightforward at first, but I can assure you, the task is anything but simple, and it's becoming more and more complex every day. As I described in Chapter 1, digital disruption is throwing the physical world of processes and goods into disorder across all industries. Marketing was among the first to get turned on its head, but fortunately, recent technological advances now enable forward-thinking organizations to regain control of today's complex digital marketing environment.

In particular, integrated marketing management (IMM), which I introduced in Chapter 3 and discussed in more detail in Chapter 10, focuses on simplifying the complexity of data, processes, interaction channels, and insights. IMM provides the tools needed to not only streamline internal workflow, but also to interact with customers and prospects in innovative and personalized ways across an ever-widening array of channels and platforms.

Without question, the days of one-way monologues directed *at* consumers are long gone. Today's marketers must engage buyers and prospects with conversations, solicit and act on customer feedback, and deliver experiences that are personalized, timely, and relevant. Not surprisingly, marketing teams have needed to add both suppliers and process steps to rise to these challenges and coordinate relatively new marketing activities, such as websites, social media, and mobile campaigns. How can marketers possibly keep all those plates spinning? They can—and they do—if they adopt a new approach. It boils down to maintaining a steady focus on the customer while implementing 21st century marketing technology.

Gartner analysts Adam Sarner and Jim Davies summed it up nicely in their 2011 paper, "Balance Customer Experience with Marketing Productivity in Marketing Automation Initiatives," when they say, "Marketing technology value comes from productivity and its impact on the customer experience. Marketers should evaluate each existing and future marketing technology based on a balance of company needs ('what's in it for us') and customer needs ('what's in it for them')."[1]

So, even as marketers concentrate on external technologies to enhance customer engagement (like integrating mobile and web for a more unified digital experience), they must improve their internal processes, as well. These internal processes must become more effective and efficient, and marketers must be able to reallocate spend from less productive to more productive parts of the marketing mix.

It truly is a delicate balancing act. To emerge from the Dark Ages into the Enlightened Age of Data, business leaders must reevaluate current systems and practices. They must look both internally and externally, and they must leverage technologies like IMM to achieve business value. After all, integration is now an essential component for business success. According to Gartner, by 2014, companies that integrate people, processes, and technology will deliver a ROMI that is 50 percent higher than those that don't.[2,3]

Clearly, IMM is the way forward. What makes the transition difficult is that it requires a mind shift—a new focus and a fresh way of thinking about marketing and what it *now* takes to succeed. As we all know, paradigm shifts take time, and no one is expecting entire systems to transform overnight. But already, I've seen compelling results from several business-to-consumer (B2C) and business-to-business (B2B) organizations that are using integrated marketing strategies to drive both internal and external value. Let me tell you how they're accomplishing their goals.

Internal Value through Integrating Marketing

Today's data-driven marketing solutions let marketers do more with less. For example, forward-thinking chief marketing officers (CMOs) are using new technologies to grab control of two broad categories of internal marketing processes: those that need to be automated, and those that can demonstrate the value of marketing activities executed. As a result, these CMOs and their teams can work faster and smarter with greater visibility.

They can see exactly what marketing dollars are being spent where, and which channels produce the highest value.

In addition, current sophisticated planning and spend management solutions let CMOs align campaign plans with organizational goals and get real-time data to manage marketing budgets. This comprehensive, coordinated approach helps eliminate misaligned marketing investments and provides better visibility and insight into the effectiveness of marketing spend across the organization. Some examples of these processes are: 1) the concept-to-plan stage of identifying a marketing opportunity and aligning resources and budget behind it, 2) the plan-to-campaign process where ideas are crystalized into a campaign with creative components like content, digital images, and 3) the creative review process to produce the components of the campaign like offers, emails, and videos, just to name a few.

Figure 11.1 shows what the modern, integrated marketing department could and should look like. Remember the fractured marketing experience we began with in Chapter 2? You have to admit, this is a whole lot more appealing.

Once companies implement data-driven solutions like these, they can achieve better control of marketing (from brand to spend), improved marketing effectiveness, more accurate measurement of return on marketing investment (ROMI), and greater marketing efficiencies.

You don't have to take my word for it. Below are several examples of how major brands have achieved internal value through integrated marketing.

Better Control of Marketing Helps Grow a National Food Brand

Over the past few years, one of the nation's premier producers, distributors, and marketers of quality food and pet products expanded rapidly through acquisitions and other growth strategies. This well-known brand owns different product lines for different consumer segments (such as organic, white label, and value-based food, to name just a few), and according to the former CMO, the company grew its brand by focusing first on individual product lines, and then managing each product to compete and win in its own category.

Initially, however, the company faced an uphill battle. It was still in the Dark Ages, burdened with a siloed, manual approach to marketing process

How does Integrated Marketing Management (IMM) benefit you?

Integrated Marketing Management is a simple solution to maintaining all of your marketing content across a global organization, and maximizing the effort of your marketing by utilizing the most advanced database technologies and continuously current customer data. Here's a look at how it works.

1 Marketing Operations

Throughout the Marketing Lifecycle, your marketing teams can better plan, create and execute campaigns. By using the most up-to-date information about how target markets are engaging, you can create a stronger, more sustainable brand relationship.

2 Digital Marketing

You can reach your customers when and where it's most convenient for them by using digital channels such as websites, email and social networks.

3 Sales and Partners

Customers receive the right message at the right time for the most optimal results. This means you receive the best possible ROI on your effort and execution.

4 Customers

Customers receive the right message at the right time for the most optimal results. This means you receive the best possible ROI on your effort and execution.

5 Marketing Analytics

Using IMM allows a broader view into how and where money is being utilized during a campaign. By constantly monitoring this against the intended ROI, you can more quickly adjust to market fluctuations.

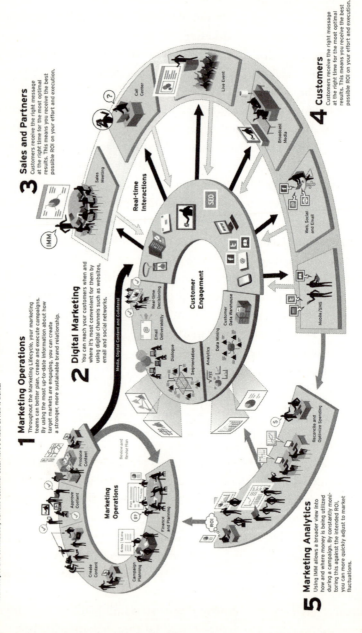

FIGURE 11.1 How Does Integrated Marketing Management (IMM) Benefit You?

Source: © Teradata 2012

154

and budgeting. In order to maintain its competitive edge, the company needed to:

1. Improve the way it planned, managed, and allocated financial and marketing resources to link programs to results.
2. Drive growth while maintaining consistent brand standards.
3. Gain visibility into growth and performance.

Integration proved to be the key to upgrading. By centralizing all marketing budgets and projects into a single platform, the marketing team was able to manage, track, and approve both entities together. The team also streamlined its practices to manage global brand standards, and then linked that back to spend.

This new approach allowed for more accountability and control for both the CMO and his marketing team. They consolidated key financial information so all departments could reference a single source of verified data, a marketing system that provides a holistic view of the marketing spend across all disparate product groups and yields complete insight into both performance results and spend.

Big Picture Marketing Drives Effectiveness at a Telecommunications Firm

When marketers are equipped with an integrated platform that manages and automates budget operations, creative processes, and campaign and product launch executions, they become more efficient and effective. They can implement proven and repeatable actions that accelerate time to market, decrease time needed to execute, and reduce wasted marketing dollars. What's more, by centralizing all the tasks, dates, deliverables, resources, *and* individuals needed to successfully complete various initiatives, marketing leaders create a global view of all activities—one they can easily monitor to ensure all projects are completed on time and on budget.

As I've already mentioned, an integrated marketing operations solution also offers a single system of record—including a formalized, cross-channel approval process—that helps align initiatives with brand requirements and business objectives. Like an electronic assembly line, each process runs with optimal timing, accuracy, cost efficiency, and transparency, and the entire cycle can be repeated upon successful completion. While the previous example demonstrated that automation and better visibility can help grow a brand, this example involves a global telecommunications company and shows how automation and better visibility improved efficiency and reduced costs.

A few years ago, this telecommunications firm faced several major road-blocks in its push to become a data-driven marketing organization. For starters, the company was fractured into nearly two dozen individual mar-kets, each of which was running its own campaigns. As you might expect, there were multiple versions of the marketing calendar, which created con-fusion between field and corporate initiatives, and there were few metrics or broader institutional knowledge of company campaigns. Fortunately, though, an integrated marketing resource management solution helped turn all that around.

How exactly did the teams at this telecommunications company use IMM technology? They standardized processes on creative development and approvals, and automated the review cycle to assure that key stakeholders were engaged and approved the campaigns on time. They also merged all the marketing activities into a central marketing calendar, providing the entire marketing organization a view of campaigns and projects.

By consolidating all the moving pieces and parts, as well as visually centralizing and providing access to the calendar, the marketers found they were able to do more marketing with less thrash—and the metrics proved that translated into real business value. By eliminating duplicate systems, the teams reduced marketing costs by more than $2 million U.S. dollars. They also reduced the time required to create and deliver key projects, sometimes by as much as two weeks! Plus, they increased their direct mar-keting efforts by 25 percent, which helped yield a significant, multimillion dollar uplift in top-line business. And the best part was that the marketing organization at this company was able to demonstrate outstanding ROMI, reflecting about 100 times the return on their integration and automation initiatives.

The marketers at this telecommunications company knew, as countless other marketers do, that the C-suite demands accountability. Now, they also know that IMM puts that once-elusive goal within their reach. By making interactions more effective and timely, marketing teams increase the chances of driving greater revenue, which is the most direct way to improve ROMI.

On a more granular level, automation gives marketers a better idea of what's working and what isn't. This allows them to continually adjust and improve the return on marketing spend. Plus, as marketing integration builds connections between team members, CMOs are able to give other managers the kind of insight they're seeking. They can show precisely how marketing is able to deliver the quantifiable results that justify the dollars they've devoted to campaign efforts.

It's extremely gratifying to untangle the big data hairball, develop more efficient processes, and prove that your marketing plan is working. Below is one of my favorite success stories from a company that did just that—across *hundreds* of different micro-markets.

More Accurate Measurement of ROMI Helps Warner Brothers Steal the Show

As a subsidiary of media giant the Time Warner Company, Warner Bros. Entertainment plays starring roles in the creation, production, distribution, licensing, and marketing of virtually every facet of the entertainment industry, including feature film, television, home entertainment, Blu-ray and DVD, digital distribution, animation, comic books, and video games. Time Warner's global brand awareness and equity transfers to Warner Bros., rendering it a chief authority in the entertainment sector and a perceptive practitioner in marketing these special products and services.

However, it became clear a few years ago that Warner Bros. had outgrown traditional manual marketing processes. The company was struggling to aggregate and execute its media campaigns with disparate information coming in from their six sister companies. The process challenges became sorely evident when media buyers tried to juggle disparate internal data with information gleaned from more than 2,500 suppliers. They needed to make quick media-spend decisions to outmarket competitors, but the process had become too complex. At first, Warner Bros. tried to rise to the challenge by focusing on media buying activities. But this approach proved to be unsustainable as global marketing became increasingly multifaceted. It was inefficient, non-scalable, and created scenarios where the answer to one problem often led to another, forcing frequent resource shifts to put out fires. Compounding these challenges, this traditional approach failed to recognize the company's need to continuously analyze the relationship between local advertising spend and box office revenues.

To clarify: The larger marketplace for Warner Bros. consists of a whopping 840 micro-markets. As you can imagine, manually generating weekly reports for these micro-markets was time-consuming and labor-intensive. Plus, by the time these reports were completed, the information was dated (and therefore inaccurate), making them largely useless for determining future spend.

After recognizing these deficiencies, the marketing team at Warner Bros. decided to implement a new approach, one that featured an integrated marketing plan coupled with spend applications that connect to sales data. The solution enabled Warner Bros. to streamline domestic media planning, placement, and purchase processes, and then, for the first time ever, to align and link these processes with finance and auditing operations.

Once its processes were aligned, Warner Bros. was able to:

- Make real-time, data-driven decisions based on spend and performance facts.
- Improve customer experience with invoices following best-practice guidelines.
- Align marketing program prioritization and performance-based plans.
- Develop and use a "single version of truth," a shared, comprehensive data source that serves as the financial system of record for marketing.
- Accelerate communication speeds.
- Predict the impacts of changes in time, scope, budget, or strategy.
- Implement and utilize a system to accumulate and store knowledge and insights based on past movie marketing campaigns, information the company can use to learn from and evolve its data strategies accordingly.

In addition, Warner Bros.' marketers have become more productive and strategic. They've eliminated repetitive, error-prone, manual tasks, such as trying to consolidate and reconcile disparate data across multiple suppliers—and, as a result, they've freed up resources for other activities.

Better Effectiveness and Efficiency in Marketing Operations Drive Value at a Global 2000 Financial Services Company

I don't want to give you the impression that B2C companies are the only ones benefiting from marketing modernization. So, here's an example of a B2B organization that improved internal marketing management to align processes, data, and financial information.

A global 2000 financial services company faced the challenge of sustaining eight separate business lines, each with its own in-house marketing team. Many of the teams' activities produced a similar end product (e.g., direct mail, pre-screen offers, collateral, etc.); however, each had different processes, making it difficult to cross-train team members or centralize support functions. With underleveraged technology, few common processes or best practices in place, and an inability to integrate support partners into their marketing, productivity shortfalls were becoming increasingly apparent.

Audits and compliance reviews were especially cumbersome and included numerous labor-intensive practices involving a combination of spreadsheets and paper files. Perhaps worst of all, the lack of marketing spend transparency prohibited the company from optimizing marketing dollars, and there were few ways for them to measure the effectiveness of marketing programs.

To resolve these growing concerns, the financial company turned to marketing operations technology, a process that may also be called marketing resource management (MRM). Since it incorporates program templates, automated workflow tools, and enhanced reporting capabilities, MRM proved to be critical to improving operational efficiencies and compliance tracking of the marketing program development processes. After implementing this solution, the company experienced impressive improvements to marketing efficiency, including:

- Centralized creative assets, approvals, and documentation.
- Best practices on collaboration and streamlined project management driven through marketing with automated workflows.
- Reduction in marketing production of cycle time by greater than five days.
- Reduction in training time for new team members by 66 percent.

Now that their processes are more efficient, the marketers at this company have more time and resources to focus on customer experience and engagement.

External Value through Integrating Marketing

There's no doubt about it: The value of big data usually delivers more excitement in its external promise to engage with more relevance than the efficiencies driven from the internal operations work necessary to elevate the marketing functions. However, as you can see from the real-world case studies I outlined in this chapter, companies must consider both internal *and* external value. There is a yin and yang relationship between the way organizations go to market and the way consumers experience a brand on the other side of the buying journey.

We've moved from a world of push marketing to one where customer-driven conversations are continuous and organic, depending upon the buyer or audience needs at that time. Marketers must now focus on integrating and streamlining the complex landscape of marketing in order to achieve this level of interaction between customer, departments, and brands, and since the industry is evolving so rapidly, anyone who wants to keep pace has no choice but to reach across traditional boundaries and start championing the changes needed to engage customers and drive revenue and differentiation. Let me tell you about a few companies that are leading the way.

Integrating Interaction Channels at a Leading Online Retailer

When business booms, the C-suite celebrates; but when a leading online retailer's domestic business began to skyrocket, the company's marketing team found the news somewhat bittersweet. Sure, more customers equated with success, but the marketers felt they couldn't keep up, and the organization began suffering frequent and painful headaches.

For instance, their outdated decision support and analytic systems made it difficult to evaluate and answer the various *what if* questions necessary to drive optimal outcomes; for example: What if we discount a product by x percent? Would that increase revenue or cut into margins? What if we ran a promotion to this segment? Would the conversions lift revenue or not? The team also had significant concerns about their email marketing application, a critical communication vehicle given the company's robust online business. Perhaps, most important of all, the marketing team realized they needed to evolve from the traditional *push* marketing model—characterized by one-way communication from the company to customers and prospects—to a *pull* marketing model that engages buyers in content and offers. The team understood this shift to pull marketing would put the brand top-of-mind when consumers decided it was time to buy.

The company's team worked with technology partners to create a single database for sales, marketing, click stream, finance, and customer service. They also modernized their campaign management applications with a robust, event-based customer relationship and interaction application that enabled them to better apply data to more relevant, timely, and personalized email promotions. The move to behavior-driven, real-time customer interaction comprised three fundamental steps:

1. The *broadcast* phase, with custom content driven by segmentation parameters and content targeting.
2. The *engage me* phase, the data-driven phase where messaging flow is driven by a mix of on-site behavior, including responses to marketing efforts that are broadcast and those that are triggered by consumer action.
3. The *empower me* phase, the behavior-driven phase in which multi-channel messaging is customized based on consumer behavior and desired value.

Modernizing and integrating key interaction channels empowered the team to enhance customer profiles and, in doing so, aid acquisition, growth, and retention efforts. Additionally, as channels became increasingly integrated, the team collected more data and shared it with colleagues so everyone could make better decisions and improve engagement strategies even more. Plus, the marketing team was also able to better align offers with customers for more efficient sales interactions.

The results were significant. By implementing IMM, this online retailer increased customer loyalty and positively impacted the bottom line. The company ultimately determined that each 1 percent of renewal rate translated to tens of millions of dollars.

Data and Integrated Marketing Drives ISC to the Winner's Circle

International Speedway Corporation (ISC) is the world's leading promoter of motor sports. The company is involved in 13 of North America's major motor sports entertainment facilities, and each year, more than 4 million fans file into ISC facilities expecting a thrilling experience. ISC aims to deliver just that, beginning with every interaction customers have before, during, and after the event—on the racetrack and off.

"If you're one of the four million fans sitting in the seats of an ISC grandstand this year, ISC wants you to feel like the experience was designed for you alone," explains Jim Cavedo, ISC's senior director of consumer marketing. "However, without a consistent, consolidated view of the customer, this vision was mere aspiration. ISC had no [singular] view across all customer campaigns; we couldn't tell you how often we touched a customer or what drove [their] purchase decision."[4]

ISC realized that in order make its goal a reality, it needed to become a "relationship marketer" instead of an "order taker." But the company's existing infrastructure wasn't set up to do this. In order to move into the Enlightened Age of Data, ISC would need to break down internal silos, replace inefficient data collection methodologies, and properly align its people for a new paradigm.

ISC has a long-standing commitment to its customers: to make them feel that the pre- and post-race experience has been specifically designed for them. Now, ISC has expanded that pledge by communicating with customers using a variety of new channels, especially social networks. The company is making it clear that customers should judge ISC by the quality of its content. So, whether it's a more streamlined newsletter, more personalized e-mail communications, or better targeted call campaigns, ISC now expects all touchpoints to and from the organization to be high-quality and deliver extraordinary value.

The complexity of ISC data was the company's largest technical challenge. There were two main issues: The data was very "dirty," with outdated, missing, or wrong information and the volume was very big. ISC realized that it could only achieve maximum value if users had confidence in the data they were analyzing. Without clean data, many conclusions would have been altered, rendering an unacceptable customer experience. ISC also needed to find a way to manage tremendous amounts of data. Because the company counts each individual seat in its stadiums as a unique product, ISC deals with an enormous volume of data (more than 13 million records). Combined with other ISC inventory, there was a staggering collection of user data dating back to 2002.

For ISC to maintain its leadership position and continue to delight shareholders, it had to continue to raise the prominence of motor sports entertainment nationally. Of course, that all starts with getting people to attend an event, and then come back to the speedway. To become a life cycle or *relationship* marketer, and effectively achieve its integrated marketing initiative targets, ISC identified three key goals:

1. Achieve a 360-degree view of each customer and prospect, including their trends, habits, and value. To achieve this, ISC continues to incorporate other sources of data, such as historic ticket sales information and merchandise sales data.
2. Enable effective segmentation and targeting (right person, right message, right time, and right channel).
3. Enhance the quality and reliability of consumer data.

ISC's marketing team worked with a core set of technology partners to build fanMAX, its interactive solution to connect with fans, and ensure that each customer receives the right communication for the right product at the right time. By creating and integrating fanMAX across people, processes, and technology, ISC has been able to change the way its business leaders think about, predict, and react to market conditions and consumer activities. As a result, ISC has been able to transform itself into a relationship marketing company and ultimately, improve marketing performance.

ISC has used state-of-the-art data collection and an integrated marketing approach to ensure that all of its fan packages are relevant to individual consumers. This translates into making sure price-conscious guests are getting offers that will appeal to their desire for value, while experience-focused fans who are less worried about cost receive offers and options that are tailored to their preferences. In addition, because every marketing initiative is started and managed through fanMAX, there is greater consistency and visibility when it comes to tracking progress. There is also increased collaboration between corporate marketing and the 13 business units (race tracks). Since implementing fanMAX, the company has accumulated more than 4 million unique customer records and 13 million orders dating back to 2002.

As Jenelle Kueter, Senior Manager of Consumer Marketing at ISC, puts it, "Data is *king*. It is absolutely how you become a more intelligent marketing organization. [We try to take every] opportunity we have to collect a little bit of data on a consumer."[5]

The company also laid out specific parameters to ensure positive customer experiences:

- ISC put **tight data governance** in place to optimize all interactive channels and avoid duplication. Since fanMAX is integrated with ISC's call center, the most up-to-date customer touchpoints are always readily available. In addition, the company "cleans" new data nightly and conducts a full database cleanse multiple times per year.
- The customer's opt-in choice **feeds directly** into the thousands of segmentations and suppressions incorporated into fanMAX.
- **Customized messaging** based on user data creates intimate communication. For example, newsletters may be based on driver preference.

As a result, an impressive *56 percent* of new customers opted in to receive track newsletters in 2010.

In addition, ISC initiated a major effort to streamline and automate over 40 marketing processes designed to facilitate collaboration across the entire company. For instance, employees must enter any job that is to use ISC marketing resources into fanMAX. This allows for immediate visibility across the entire company, which, in turn, enables people to prioritize and correctly allocate resources.

Although ISC's specific budget numbers are confidential, the initial project and the annual costs were returned in the first year (2009) just through prospecting success alone. The company maintained similar results in 2010 and expects to continue improving the process, time to market, and ROMI each year. Additional gains include:

- **Expansion in email campaigns** from 250 in 2007 to more than 1,000 today.
- **Management of more than 5,000 total marketing projects.**
- **Uplift in campaigns and attendance.** ISC created 2,400 segments in a micro-segmentation approach that invigorated their fan base and improved engagement.
- **Reductions in time to market.** Senior management reported automated processes and streamlined workflow cut time to market in half.

- **Improved workflow.** ISC also enabled and trained representatives of the racetracks to design, edit, and send their own emails, instead of pushing those jobs through corporate services. Although the business units currently take the lead on developing marketing messages, they will gain the ability to own the entire process for the bulk of their simpler communications. This will then free up corporate services to focus on more complex communications and campaigns, as well as the analytics to support the business moving forward.

Gartner awarded ISC the CRM Excellence Award in the Integrated Marketing category at its 2011 Customer 360 Summit, and the Ventana Research 2013 Business Technology Leadership Award in Marketing Excellence. By winning awards in these categories, ISC was recognized for its success in integrating people, processes, and technologies across the marketing ecosystem to increase effectiveness, improve efficiency, and drive marketing performance and ROMI.

KEY TERMS

Marketing resource management (MRM): A process and approach to achieve marketing success. MRM contains marketing operations functionality that manages:
- Planning and financials
- Production management and workflow
- Offer management
- Brand assets, both digital and physical
- Localization and distribution of collateral and advertising
- Project management
- Dynamic calendars

Customer interaction management: Combines powerful analytics with automated customer communication capabilities to drive relevant and timely messages into operational systems, allowing you to interact intelligently with your customers.

DOs AND DON'Ts

Look internally and externally. Analyze processes with both customers and employees to understand your biggest obstacles and what might be holding you back. Remember: Your goal is to integrate marketing and use big data insights across the enterprise so you can drive value by engaging customers more effectively.

Leverage best practices. Upgrading your marketing operations, customer interaction management, and overall go-to-market strategy is an enormous endeavor, so take it one step at a time. Visualize your future state, and then work with proven experts to begin adopting a more data-driven marketing approach.

Learn from the efforts of others. There's no need to reinvent the wheel every time. As we've seen from this chapter and the others preceding it, many companies have tackled big data marketing to become data-driven organizations with successful results. But don't forget: Marketing is constantly evolving. Read, listen, talk, and network. Apply the best of what you learn—and avoid the land mines others point out—to transform your own business and organization.

Don't kid yourself. Be honest about your current position. A holistic vision and understanding of where your team *truly* is will provide the best foundation for moving forward.

Don't let the complexity grow. Complexity is one of the biggest obstacles marketers face. And if you think it's bad today, just wait—it's only going to get more complicated in the future. Work with IT and your peers to understand where complexity can be eliminated and where simplification and streamlining can be adopted. Ensure that, as you add new technologies and processes, you take the time to look back at the impact.

12

The Bright, Enlightened World of Customer Experience

For decades science fiction movies have captured audiences imaginations—maybe because they allow us, for at least a few hours, to peer into the possibilities of the future. The high-tech gadgetry, biometric security features, interactive 3-D holograms, and vast information management systems that once seemed only possible on the silver screen are now becoming part of our daily lives—and marketers are at the forefront of these major technological and cultural shifts.

In 2013, McKinsey & Company painted its own picture of the future: an "on-demand world where consumers will judge brands by their ability to deliver heightened experiences—interactions, literally anywhere, that offer high levels of value and are radically customized and easy to access—along the consumer decision journey."[1] In the report, McKinsey envisions mobile phones exchanging information with durable products like headsets and gym equipment to engage and empower peer-to-peer commerce. Interactions like these are already beginning to happen, and in the near future, these tools could be even more integral in managing consumer buying behavior, interacting with each other for upsell and cross-sell, and serving as the consumer's constant companion.

Will I be able to walk though a mall someday and see personalized advertisements appear on the walls, all perfectly correlated to my mental state (as in Steven Spielberg's film *Minority Report*)? Naturally, no one knows for sure, but we *do* know this: Technology is transforming our society in profound ways, and I see these changes falling into four broad categories: 1) people, 2) mobile devices, 3) information management, and 4) big data. Each has its own challenges and opportunities, which I'll explore throughout this chapter.

The People Marketing Challenge

People are becoming increasingly connected. In his book, *Digital Wisdom: Thought Leadership for a Connected World*, technology expert Shelly Palmer discusses how quickly technology is changing the world.[2] To describe the exponential growth, he references award-winning inventor and futurist Ray Kurzweil's concept "the law of accelerating returns." This law of evolving technology was described in Kurzweil's book *The Singularity Is Near: When Humans Transcend Biology*.[3] Palmer cites Kurzweil's prophetic quote: "We won't experience 100 years of progress in the 21st century—it will be more like 20,000 years of progress (at today's rate) because the pace of technological change is exponential."[4]

We've witnessed technology's ability to connect people through social networks, smartphones, and personal video conferencing. It makes sense to assume that we will see a parallel acceleration and expansion of human connectedness as technology accelerates. For example, a growing number of consumers will check in with peers before making buying decisions. Meanwhile, technology will get easier and more intuitive to use, and that will eliminate barriers to interaction. As a result, people will connect with larger networks, faster, and more frequently than they do today.

People—especially leaders—will need to manage change, *fast*. Business leaders of the past were recognized and rewarded for their special knowledge and skills in specific, well-defined areas. Even as little as five years ago, you needed to become a domain expert of some sort if you wanted to get ahead, but leadership qualities are being assessed differently today. To succeed in the business environment of the future, leaders will need to be collaborators, people who can work with others to continually expand their skill sets, innovate, and find solutions.

Moreover, these future leaders will be evaluated on their ability to *seek change*. Anyone who wants to climb the corporate ladder will have to embrace and drive the change required to improve the customer experience and deliver business growth. One of my current favorite examples of change in action is the work that Marissa Mayer is leading at Yahoo!. As I'm writing this book, Mayer is leading Yahoo!'s turnaround and, according to Seeking Alpha, a platform for financial research, she and her team have driven a 72 percent growth in the stock price year over year.[5] In addition to the shareholder growth, Mayer has taken big steps to revitalize the Yahoo! brand, champion the acquisition of Tumblr, expand the company's content arsenal, and make some difficult calls, such as retracting the generous work-at-home culture of Yahoo!. Mayer, a first-time CEO, is a change agent focused on improving Yahoo!'s appeal to the market.

The People Marketing Opportunity

There is vast opportunity for marketers within these changing dynamics of human interaction, but before seizing any opportunities, marketers must first develop trust with consumers. They need to learn to build smart interactions by offering value-added content and experiences, not spam and strong-arming. Imagine a bank that lets you in on all the information they know about you—your credit score, your credit threshold, and so on—and, in turn, empowers you to make buying decisions faster and more autonomously. Exchanges like these empower the consumer to connect, while minimizing the inconvenience and effort required to transact, communicate, or enjoy products, services, and brands.

The Mobile Marketing Challenge

Smartphones will become smarter . . . and smarter . . . and smarter. Given how many of us are already tethered to our smartphones, it may be somewhat difficult for you to envision, but in the future, we will become even more dependent on mobile devices. We will leverage these personal, portable, digital ecosystems not only to communicate with fellow humans, but also to interact with other machines and devices to communicate, transact, and remember. We've already seen phones in the retail environment turned into point-of-sale systems, accelerating a transaction, and making it easier for consumers to buy on the spot. Imagine the future when your phone connects with a sensor in the supermarket, reads your shopping list, and provides you a map to speed your trip through the store. How else will emerging technologies ease the path to purchase? Without question, mobile devices are *the* communication channel, and marketers are already using geo-location technology to improve the customer experience. Marketers strive to deliver the right message to the right person at the right time, and what better time could there possibly be than at the point of purchase? Mobile devices allow you to communicate with customers before and when they're ready to buy.

Walmart understands the potential of mobile. As *Mobile Commerce Daily* reported, Walmart won the prestigious Mobile Retailer of the Year for 2012.[6] Walmart was recognized for various innovations, including:

- **Scan & Go.** This app saves shoppers time by allowing them to scan items with their iPhone, bag the purchases while they shop, and use seamless payment to bypass the lines at check-out. By March of 2013, Walmart had already expanded this service to more than 200 stores in the United States.
- **Store Mode.** This app detects when consumers enter a store location using geo-location and geo-fencing technology.
- **Price checking.** Walmart shoppers can use mobile devices to check product prices.
- **Shopping lists and discounts.** Shoppers can use mobile devices to plan and manage shopping lists, store and use digital coupons, and scan QR codes.

Location information will become even more pervasive as more and more of these smart devices capture and aggregate geographically located information. But before consumers enable location tracking, they will want assurances that retailers and brands will be good stewards of data related to their whereabouts. The battle for consumer trust will take precedence, and ultimately, it will allow relationship marketers and brands to achieve targeted narrowcasting of offers and experiences.

One-way communications will continue to fade away. Email is a perfect example of a once-powerful communication channel that ended up disenfranchising consumers because of the volume of irrelevant, one-way messages so many companies and brands send. What can marketers learn from email's fate? How can you apply those lessons to the digital channels of the future? Marketers probably won't need retinal scans to succeed, but we *will* need a holistic view of the target receiver and enough content and offers to satisfy their needs and wants. Savvy marketers will stop using traditional marketing tactics; instead, they'll learn to build synergistic relationships with their buyers. They won't use big data insights to do creepy things, like stalk consumers online, but they will use their powers to enrich the consumer experience and add value in the process. To be able to deliver on this promise and enjoy the results of delighting and improving the lives of their customers, today's marketers need to begin redefining their marketing approaches. As I've talked about throughout this book, they'll need to untangle the data hairball to be able to apply information in a meaningful way that adds value to both consumers and companies.

The Mobile Marketing Opportunity

Technology already lets marketers track the customer journey. Mobile devices will further transform future interactions with your consumers, prospects, and buyers, and they will very likely serve as the primary conduit to improving the customer experience. Combining mobile technology with big data analytics creates powerful possibilities and will help marketers provide truly individual, personalized communications. While true one-to-one relationships have been the Holy Grail for marketing for more than 20 years, marketers are still utilizing segmentation and micro segments to enhance and deliver relevant messages. But, true one-to-one marketing is about a relationship between a brand and a single consumer. I'm seeing digital marketers move to embrace digital marketing attribution—the ability to understand an individual—as the next step towards markets of one. It's essential to identify correlations in behavior, preference, and supplemental data to take personalization further.

What are the next steps for your company? Proceed thoughtfully. Ask questions like: What adds value to your target customer *at this very moment*? How can your company enhance the experience, content, or interaction you already provide to improve that consumer's life, buying experience, or world?

The Information Management Marketing Challenge

Consumers will control information access. While science fiction is full of examples in which the government or marketers control the public's experiences and choices, I don't see that happening in our future. Instead, I believe individuals will manage their data better, and they'll determine how much of it they want to share with companies. Indeed, we have already seen consumers exert more control leveraging privacy options on social networks and other access to information dissemination.

Think about it. When I was developing growth strategies for my employer a few years ago, a mentor of mine told me, "Follow the money." So, let's do that. The government doesn't have the money. Corporations do, but their margins are getting squeezed year after year after year. If we truly follow the money, it leads straight to the consumer. They are where the buying power lies *and* where the information will be the most relevant.

I can imagine a day when each of us manages all our private data—and not just the basics, like our age and our address. We'll also have more direct control over our credit ratings, our personal health data, and information about our buying and consumption behavior. We will each have a personal information management system that can connect with brands and companies through sensor tags on the things we buy and through the optional transmission of information in exchange for something we value. In its early stages of development, persona management will emerge with the consumer calling the shots.

The company will own the customer data. Turf wars will eventually exhaust corporate executives, and the stakes will be too high to ignore the growing big data hairball. As companies unravel this knot of digital information, they will build internal processes, governance, and systems to manage, scale, and secure data consolidated across all channels, departments, interactions, and parties. No longer will a single department be able to claim that it owns the customer data; it will be clear that the enterprise holds ownership of this precious lifeblood of information.

The Information Marketing Opportunity

When marketers fully understand the customer's buying journey and all its touchpoints, they're able to construct meaningful interactions that exchange information, offers, messages, and services that add value. So, why not begin developing these insights today? If you start indoctrinating a culture and nurturing a trusted relationship with the consumer now, you'll pave the way for future gains.

The Big Data Marketing Challenge ━━━━

Data scientists in marketing are not unicorns. Unicorns are elusive, magical creatures that everyone would love to find, but no one has ever seen. Data scientists are not such mythical beings; but between 2013 and 2016, data scientists may seem elusive and magical to the marketers in need of their quantitative and business skills. Virtually all C-level executives want to build their teams' analytical skills, and even though we'll see more and more data scientists in marketing, there will likely be a shortage of them in the short term. These talented individuals are able to balance and understand both business and advanced analytics, which makes them perfect for the job of the chief marketing officer's (CMO's) first mate. They'll help CMOs discover new trends and new paths to revenue. As our industry matures, future marketers and C-level execs will be expected to have analytical skills and critical thinking in addition to brand knowledge.

I also predict that the role of CMO will either expand or evolve. Marketing as a key business function will continue to transform to become a department for data-driven customer-engagement. Alternatively, marketing might be decentralized and incorporated into other core functions like sales, service, and operations. We will see marketing executives who are either sales- or customer-focused, and brand CMOs will become the rarest breed.

The Big Data Marketing Opportunity ━━━━

It's time we call a halt to the goat rodeos in our boardrooms. Our opportunity to do that begins now. Let's not make the same mistakes we made during the dot.com bubble where we didn't dig in, understand, or hypothesize. We didn't seize the opportunity the new online commerce space offered to all industries and businesses. As a result, we now stand on the edge of industry-wide disruption. Data-driven marketing powered by big data insights is just one area where focus, funding, and experimentation could be the inflection point your business is seeking.

Ironically, we have the opportunity to be so effective with big data marketing that we work ourselves out of the jobs we have today. Perhaps in the future, marketers, data scientists, and interaction strategies won't exist, and machines will conduct our marketing work invisibly, using data as naturally as we use intelligence. These machines will engage and involve us; they'll know what we want. This network of things, sensors, and machines will use data with our permission to really get to *understand* us; and our homes, cars, and workplaces will be able to predict and facilitate our behaviors.

Today, data is a bit of a nemesis, but in time, we will tame it. We'll come to see data as an ally, and we'll use it to do beautiful, helpful things. We'll take data to a place where marketing is no longer something coming *at* us, but something that is part *of* us and the human faculty of moment-to-moment decision-making. This is our opportunity—the opportunity of big data marketing.

Notes

Chapter 1 Moving Out of the Dark Ages

1. Palmer, Shelly. *Digital Wisdom: Thought Leadership for a Connected World*. Stamford: York House, 2013.
2. Schwartz, Julie. "ITSMA's 2011 Online Survey on Data Driven Marketing," April 28, 2011. Online reference. http://www.itsma.com/research/data-driven-survey-2011/.
3. Teradata Corporation. 2013 Teradata Data-Driven Marketing Survey, Global. August 5, 2013. Research report, http://www.teradata.com/data-driven-market ing/market-research-results-2013/.
4. *Teradata Magazine* online. "Case Study: DSW: If the Shoe Fits, Sell It!," 2012. Online reference. http://www.teradatamagazine.com/v12n02/Features/If-the-Shoe-Fits,-Sell-It!/.
5. Laney, Doug. *Meta Delta Application Delivery Strategies*. "3D Data Management: Controlling Data Volume, Velocity, and Variety." January 2012. Online reference. http://blogs.gartner.com/doug-laney/files/2012/01/ad949–3D-Data-Management-Controlling-Data-Volume-Velocity-and-Variety.pdf.

Chapter 2 Why Is Marketing Antiquated?

1. Aprimo-Teradata. "'Showrooming' by Consumers Using Mobile Devices Is Transforming Retail Shopping" (press release). November 15, 2012.
2. RightNow Technologies. "Customer Experience Report, North America." 2010. Online reference. http://www.rightnow.com/files/analyst-reports/RightNow-Customer-Experience-Impact-North-America-Report.pdf.
3. Dimensional Research. "Customer Service and Business Results: A Survey of Customer Service from Mid-size Companies." April 2013. http://cdn.zendesk .com/resources/whitepapers/Zendesk_WP_Customer_Service_and_Business _Results.pdf.
4. Teradata Corporation. "BARC Big Data Survey: Lack of Experts and Know-how a Main Obstacle to Monetizing Big Data" (press release). April 11, 2013. Online reference. http://www.teradata.com/News-Releases/2013/BARC-Big-Data-Survey-Lack-of-Experts-and-Know-how-A-Main-Obstacle-to-Monetizing-Big-Data/.

5. Teradata Corporation. "Solving the Jobs Gap for Big Data Analytics Careers Requires Access to Cutting-Edge Technology and Big Data: Survey" (press release). April 29, 2013. Online reference. http://www.teradata.com/News-Releases/2013/Solving-the-Jobs-Gap-for-Big-Data-Analytics-Careers-Requires-Access-to-Cutting-Edge-Technology-and-Big-Data-Survey/.

6. Teradata Corporation. 2013 Teradata Data-Driven Marketing Survey, Global. August 5, 2013. Research report, http://www.teradata.com/data-driven-market ing/market-research-results-2013/.

Chapter 3   The Data Hairball

1. Teradata Corporation. 2013 Teradata Data-Driven Marketing Survey, Global. August 5, 2013. Research report, http://www.teradata.com/data-driven-market ing/market-research-results-2013/.

2. Manning, Harley. *Harley Manning's Blog*, "Customer Experience Defined." Forrester Blogs: November 23, 2010. Online reference. http://blogs.forrester .com/harley_manning/10–11–23-customer_experience_defined.

3. Shaw, Colin, Qaalfa Dibeehi, and Steven Walden. *Customer Experience: Future Trends and Insights*. Palgrave Macmillan, October 2010, p. 3.

4. Teradata Corporation. Case Study "ISC Builds Relationship Marketing Platform that Integrates People, Processes and Technologies." 2011.

5. Peggy Dyer (CMO of American Red Cross), interviews by Lisa B. Arthur, Indianapolis, IN, 2012–2013.

6. Linda Woolley (CEO of Direct Marketing Association), interview by Lisa B. Arthur, Indianapolis, IN, 2013.

7. Quoted in. Salls, Manda, and Sean Silverthorne. *Harvard Business School Working Knowledge*, "Should You Sell Your Digital Privacy?" August 25, 2003. Online reference. http://hbswk.hbs.edu/item/3636.html.

Chapter 4   Definitions for the Real World of Big Data Marketing

1. Teradata Corporation. "Empowering Data-Driven Marketing: Teradata Introduces "Interactive Customer Engagement" (press release). April 9, 2013. Online reference. http://www.teradata.com/News-Releases/2013/Teradata-Intro duces-Interactive-Customer-Engagement/.

2. Teradata Corporation. Global Teradata Data Driven Marketing Survey, 2013.

3. McClellan, Laura. "By 2017 the CMO will Spend More on IT Than the CIO." Gartner Webinar, January 3, 2012. http://my.gartner.com/portal/server.pt?open =512&objID=202&mode=2&PageID=5553&resId=1871515.

4. Laney, Doug. *Meta Delta Application Delivery Strategies*. "3D Data Management: Controlling Data Volume, Velocity, and Variety." January 2012. Online

reference. http://blogs.gartner.com/doug-laney/files/2012/01/ad949–3D-Data-Management-Controlling-Data-Volume-Velocity-and-Variety.pdf.

5. Cloud Partners. "Facebook Users Upload 100 Terabytes of Data Daily," Blog post. March 28, 2012. Online reference. http://www.cloudpartnerstm.com/facebook-users-upload-100-terab/wsdindex.html.

6. Gantz, John, and David Reinsel. "The Digital Universe in 2020: Big Data, Bigger Digital Shadows, and Biggest Growth in the Far East." IDC Corporation, sponsored by EMC Corporation, December 2012.

7. Sarner, Adam. "Digital Marketing: A Transformational Approach for Marketers." Gartner Webinar, September 25, 2012. Online reference. http://my.gartner.com/portal/server.pt?open=512&objID=202&mode=2&PageID=5553&ref=webinar-rss&resId=2090115.

Chapter 5 Meet The Modern Marketing Department (Michelangelo Meets Einstein)

1. SpencerStuart. "Chief Marketing Office Tenure Now at 45 Months" (press release). May 1, 2013. Online reference http://www.spencerstuart.com/about/media/77/.

2. Wizdo, Lori. "Buyer Behavior Helps B2B Marketers Guide the Buyer's Journey." Forrester Blogs, October 4, 2012. Online reference. http://blogs.forrester.com/lori_wizdo/12–10–04-buyer_behavior_helps_b2b_marketers_guide_the_buyers_journey.

3. Goden, Seth. *Linchpin: Are You Indispensible.* New York: Penguin Group, 2010.

4. Heath, Chip and Dan. *Switch: How to Drive Change When Change is Hard.* New York: Random House, 2011.

5. Davenport, Thomas, and D. J. Patil. *Harvard Business Review*, "Data Scientist: The Sexiest Job of the 21st Century." October 2012.

6. Teradata Aster. "Data Scientist: IT or Business? Or Both?" Accessed June 25, 2013. Online reference. http://www.asterdata.com/resources/video-data-scientist.php.

7. McGuire, Tim. McKinsey's Chief Marketing & Sales Officer Forum, "Marketing & IT in the Age of Big Data." December 2012. Online reference. http://cmsoforum.mckinsey.com/article/marketing-it-in-the-age-of-big-data.

8. Quoted in Edwards, John. *Teradata Magazine* online, "Digital Destiny: To Stay Competitive, Enterprises Look to the Chief Digital Officer to Lead Them into the Future." Q3 2012. Online reference. http://www.teradatamagazine.com/v12n03/Features/Digital-Destiny/.

9. Berkman, Robert. *MIT Sloan Management Review* blog, "The Emergence of Chief Digital Officers." April 29, 2013. Online reference. http://sloanreview.mit.edu/article/social-business-helps-usher-in-new-executive-the-cdo/.

10. Quoted in Arthur, Lisa. *Forbes*, "A Guide to Surviving Today's Business Gauntlet." January 11, 2012. Online reference. http://www.forbes.com/sites/lisaarthur/2012/01/11/a-guide-to-surviving-todays-business-gauntlet/.

Chapter 6 Step One: Get Smart, Get Strategic

1. *CustomersThink* blog, "Why CRM Fails." January 30, 2011. Online reference. http://www.crm-guru.com/why-crm-fails.php.
2. Davenport, Tom, in an interview with Gary Beach, Enterprise CIO Forum, "Dawn of the Data Scientist." November 19, 2013.
3. Strum, Jim. 2013 e-mail interview by Lisa B. Arthur, Indianapolis, IN, 2013.
4. PricewaterhouseCoopers. "5th Annual Digital IQ Survey: Digital Conversations and the C-Suite." 2013.

Chapter 7 Step Two: Tear Down the Silos

1. Gulati, Ranjay. *Harvard Business Review*, "The Four Cs of Customer-Focused Solutions." 2007. Online reference. http://hbr.org/web/special-collections/insight/customers/silo-busting-how-to-execute-on-the-promise-of-customer-focus.
2. PricewaterhouseCoopers. "5th Annual Digital IQ Survey: Digital Conversations and the C-Suite." 2013.
3. David Bonalle (Head of Marketing and Customer Insights at Key Bank) interview. Cleveland, Ohio. 2013.

Chapter 8 Step Three: Untangle the Data Hairball

1. Jeffrey Hayzlett (Contributing Editor, Bloomberg and former Kodak CMO), interviews by Lisa B. Arthur, Indianapolis, IN, 2013.
2. Peggy Dyer (CMO of American Red Cross), interviews by Lisa B. Arthur, Indianapolis, IN, 2012–2013.
3. Bladt, Jeff, and Bob Filbin. *Harvard Business Review* blog, "A Data Scientist's Real Job: Storytelling." March 27, 2013. Online reference. blogs.hbr.org/cs/2013/03/a_data_scientists_real_job_sto.html.
4. Franks, Bill. *Harvard Business Review* blog, "To Succeed with Big Data, Start Small." October 3, 2012. Online reference. http://blogs.hbr.org/cs/2012/10/to_succeed_with_big_data_start.html.
5. Bladt, Jeff, and Bob Filbin. *Harvard Business Review* blog, "A Data Scientist's Real Job: Storytelling." March 27, 2013. Online reference. blogs.hbr.org/cs/2013/03/a_data_scientists_real_job_sto.html.

Chapter 9 Step Four: Make Metrics Your Mantra

1. Bose, Gautam. *Teradata Magazine* online. "Customer Relations Best Practices." Q3 2012. Online reference. http://www.teradatamagazine.com/v12n03/Connections/5-Customer-Relations-Best-Practices/.
2. Lenskold Group and Aprimo. "The CMO Guide to Marketing ROI." 2010.
3. Palda, Kristian S. *The Measurement of Cumulative Advertising Effects*. Englewood Cliffs, NJ: Prentice Hall, 1964.
4. Gary Lilien, Philip Kotler, and K.Sridhar Moorthy, *Marketing Models*. Prentice Hall, 1991.
5. Lenskold Group and Aprimo. "The CMO Guide to Marketing ROI." 2012–2013.
6. Crandell, Christine. Blog post and interview with Lisa Arthur. Blogs and post interview via e-mail June 2013. www.christinecrandell.com.
7. Petralia, John. Keynote given at Marketing Science Institute Conference: Marketing Resource Allocation: From Analytics to Insight 2013. University of Virginia, Charlottesville, VA. 2013.
8. Nadolny, Mark. SiriusDecisions blog, "Price Check: Marketing Cost per Lead." January 29, 2013. Online reference. http://www.siriusdecisions.com/blog/price-check-marketing-cost-per-lead/.

Chapter 10 Step Five: Process Is the New Black

1. http://www.businessdictionary.com/definition/business-process.html.
2. Kotler, Philip. *Marketing Management: Analysis, Planning, and Control*. Prentice Hall, 1967.
3. Collins, Kimberly. "The Four New Ps of Marketing that CMOs and CIOs Should Consider." Gartner, May 18, 2012.
4. Ibid.
5. Borgias, Brooke, and John F. Tanner Jr. "Hyper-Accelerated Marketing Operations: The Focus on the Family Campaign John 3:16." Baylor University, 2012.
6. 2013 Teradata Data-Driven Marketing Survey, Global. August 5, 2013. Research report, http://www.teradata.com/data-driven-marketing/market-research-results-2013/.
7. http://www.agilemarketing.net/what-is-agile-marketing/.

Chapter 11 Drive Value through Relevant Marketing

1. Davies, Jim, and Adam Sarner. "Balance Customer Experience with Marketing Productivity in Marketing Automation Initiatives." Gartner, September 2, 2011.

2. Collins, Kimberly, and Adam Sarner. "Magic Quadrant for Enterprise Marketing Management." Gartner, October 14, 2010.

3. Collins, Kimberly. "Focus on Integrated (Rather Than Enterprise) Marketing Management." Gartner, October 6, 2010.

4. Teradata Corporation. Case Study "ISC builds relationship marketing platform that integrates people, processes and technologies." 2011.

5. Interview follow-up to case study via e-mail, June 2013.

Chapter 12   The Bright, Enlightened World of Customer Experience

1. Dahlstrom, Peter, and David Edelman. "The Coming Era of 'On-demand' Marketing." McKinsey & Company, April 2013.

2. Palmer, Shelly. *Digital Wisdom: Thought Leadership for a Connected World.* Stamford: York House Press, 2012.

3. Kurzweil, Ray. *The Singularity Is Near: When Humans Transcend Biology.* The Viking Press, 2005.

4. Quoted in Palmer, Shelly. *Digital Wisdom: Thought Leadership for a Connected World.* Stamford: York House Press, 2012.

5. Lemmola, Elisa. "With Marissa Mayer at the Helm, Is Yahoo Stock Now a Smart Buy?" *Seeking Alpha.* June 2, 2013. Online reference. http://seekingalpha .com/article/1475231-with-marissa-mayer-at-the-helm-is-yahoo-stock-now-a-smart-buy?source=yahoo.

6. Katz, Rimma. "Walmart Is Mobile Retailer of the Year," *Mobile Commerce Daily.* December 31, 2012. Online reference. http://www.mobilecommercedaily.com/ walmart-is-mobile-retailer-of-the-year.

Resources

www.teradata.com/big-data-marketing

or

www.bigdatamarketingbook.com

- The Top Five Myths of Big Data Analytics: What Every Marketing Leader Needs to Know (White paper)
- Overview of Data Driven Marketing (White paper)
- 2013 Teradata Data-Driven Marketing Survey, EMEA
- 2013 Teradata Data-Driven Marketing Survey, Global
- The New CMO-CIO Alignment: Best Practices for Driving Collaboration Between Marketing and IT (White paper)
- Teradata Marketing Maturity Assessment (White paper)
- Using Data to Drive Marketing Results and a Sustainable Competitive Advantage (White paper)
- Customer Centricity (White paper)
- Data-Driven: How Marketers Profit from Technology in a Multi-Channel World (Report)
- The Impact of Creating an Integrated Marketing Management Environment on the Customer Experience (White paper)
- Using Multi-Touch Attribution for Deeper Insight into the Customer Journey: Welcome to the Era of Digital Intelligence (White paper)
- Ten Steps To Turn Customer Data Into A Competitive Edge (2-part Blog Series)
- Big Data Marketing Hero (e-book)

Industry Content

- How to Put Data and Analytics to Work in the Era of Healthcare Reform Demonstrated by Blue Cross Blue Shield of North Carolina (White paper)

- Healthcare's Future Depends on Data-Driven Insights into Individual Behavior (White paper)
- IDC-Perspective: HealthPlan CRM-Driving Consumer Value into the Customer Relationship (Analyst Report)

Infographics

- Data-Driven Marketing Customer Journey
- Integrated Marketing Management
- The Top Five Myths of Big Data Analytics: What Every Marketing Leader Needs to Know
- Great Minds Don't Always Think Alike: the New CIO + CMO Strategic Alignment
- The Growing Trend of Showrooming

Case Studies

- Bank of America
- Bouygues Telecom
- Cummins
- Designer Shoe Warehouse (DSW) Video
- International Speedway Corporation (ISC)
- Nationwide: Delivering an On Your Side Experience
- Warner Brothers

About the Author

Lisa Arthur is a four-time chief marketing officer (CMO) who has been on the front lines of technology marketing for more than 30 years. As the CMO of Teradata Applications, Arthur serves as an industry thought leader, meeting and speaking regularly with CMOs and marketing teams from today's most iconic brands to discuss integrated marketing management (IMM), data-driven marketing, and marketing innovation. She founded Cinterim, a Silicon Valley marketing strategy and consulting firm that catered to start-ups and Fortune 50 companies; served as CMO of Internet leader, Akamai Technologies, where she helped put the company on a path to billion-dollar revenue; and enjoyed seven years as a vice president of marketing at Oracle, where she managed the company's market entry and growth for customer relationship management (CRM). Arthur has published over 100 articles in *Forbes* for the CMO Network as well as other industry magazines about how big data and data-driven marketing are changing business. When not on a plane, Arthur lives in Indianapolis, Indiana, with her husband and their cat, Tiki. Follow Lisa on Twitter, @lisaarthur, to join in on the conversation.

Index